Leahy

Workers' Compensation System in Michigan

A Closed Case Survey

H. ALLAN HUNT

The W. E. Upjohn Institute
for Employment Research

Library of Congress Cataloging in Publication Data

Hunt, H. Allan.
    Workers' compensation system in Michigan.

   1. Workers' compensation—Michigan.   I. Title.
HD7103.65.U6H864   1982   368.4'1'009774   82-20250
ISBN 0-88099-005-8 (pbk.)

THE INSTITUTE, a nonprofit research organization, was established on July 1, 1945. It is an activity of the W. E. Upjohn Unemployment Trustee Corporation, which was formed in 1932 to administer a fund set aside by the late Dr. W. E. Upjohn for the purpose of carrying on "research into the causes and effects of unemployment and measures for the alleviation of unemployment."

Foreword

This study of the workers' compensation system in Michigan, initiated in 1978, has already achieved one of its major objectives: to provide a needed data base for analyzing the complex and often controversial workers' compensation issues. The data gathered for this study were frequently utilized during the period of reform activity which resulted in the 1980 and 1981 amendments.

While the amendments enacted in 1980 and 1981 have substantially altered Michigan's system, this study provides an empirical overview of workers' compensation cases in the state that has not been available before. As a quantitative picture of the system in 1978, a point prior to any statutory changes, it may prove useful as a benchmark for assessing the impact of amendments to the statute.

Facts and observations presented in this monograph are the sole responsibility of the author. The viewpoints do not necessarily represent positions of the W. E. Upjohn Institute for Employment Research.

Jack R. Woods
Acting Director

November 1982

Executive Summary

The Michigan Closed Case Survey consists of data abstracted from 2,200 litigated and unlitigated workers' compensation cases closed in the Fall of 1978. This monograph is a description of that data base. It attempts to accomplish three major objectives: (1) to provide a comparative analysis of the workers' compensation experience of the insured and self-insured employer populations; (2) to provide an empirical description of the workers' compensation system in Michigan; and (3) to examine the differences between litigated and unlitigated cases with the goal of understanding the role of litigation in the Michigan workers' compensation system.

Perhaps the study's greatest contribution is the comparative analysis of workers' compensation cases from insured employers and self-insured employers, further divided into the big three auto manufacturers and all other self-insureds. The basic finding is that these three employer types have very different workers' compensation experiences. It was not possible to document this before the Michigan Closed Case Survey since no single data base included both insured and self-insured employers.

These differences are demonstrated most dramatically in the proportion of cases litigated. Among the workers' compensation cases from employees of the big three auto producers, 48 percent are litigated. Other self-insured employers experience 19 percent and insured employers a 22 percent litigation rate. The differences in proportion of cases litigated in turn produce vast contrasts in claimant characteristics, the type and amount of compensation paid, and the timeliness of payments by insurer type.

The importance of the litigation process was also demonstrated in the magnitude of lump-sum payments in Michigan's workers' compensation system. Some 60 percent of all indemnity payments to this sample of closed cases were made in the form of lump-sums. Proportions by insurer type varied from 67 percent for the big three to 54 percent for other self-insurers. The insured population fell in between, with 61 percent lump-sums. Retired claimants were estimated to be receiving 10 percent of all indemnity for the insured population, 40 percent for the big three, and 20 percent for other self-insurers. Lump-sum indemnity payments were shown to vary directly with earnings level and weekly compensation payments. They also were related to the number of periods of disability, hospitalization, back injuries, and the type of insurer.

This study also provides an empirical overview of workers' compensation cases in the State of Michigan that has not been available before. Simple descriptive facts such as the weekly benefit levels, durations of disability, characteristics of claimants, and many others are discussed. These data are organized by insurer type, so this general description also has a comparative flavor. Thus, when lump-sum payments and weekly payments are considered together, it is demonstrated that the big three and the insured employers have very similar average disability durations, but other self-insured employers enjoy average durations some 30 percent lower.

Analysis of the weekly benefit levels also proved very interesting. The wage replacement formula operates in such a way that only 20 percent of beneficiaries actually received the two-thirds gross replacement rate specified by statute. This reflects the maximum and minimum benefit levels, dependency allowances, and other administrative factors. The result is that 15 percent of Michigan's workers' compensation claimants received less than 40 percent gross wage replacement, while 3 percent received over 100 percent and another 10 percent received between 70 and 100 percent gross wage replacement rates.

The review of the role of litigation in Michigan's workers' compensation system led to the general conclusion that the litigated and unlitigated cases should be regarded as operating in two separate systems. They operate with different procedures, on different time schedules, with different outcomes, and to a surprising extent with different claimants. While the unlitigated system operates as a wage-loss replacement mechanism for disabled workers, the litigated system does not appear to operate on the same set of principles.

The evidence presented in the study suggests that Michigan's workers' compensation litigation system has grown into a miniature replica of the tort liability system of 70 years ago, the system that workers' compensation was supposed to replace. The major difference is that disputes over who is at fault have been replaced by disputes over what is at fault. The lump-sum settlement system is seen as encouraging claims from retirees while driving out other, more timely, disputed cases. A general overhaul of the litigation system in workers' compensation is urged.

Acknowledgments

There are a number of people who have been critical to the completion of this study at various points over the past four years. I would begin with Beth Zechinato and Jo Walker of the Bureau of Workers' Disability Compensation who accommodated the data collection effort with good humor even though they were under considerable pressure. Thanks are also owed to Betty Newhouse, Norma Tubbs, Marge Mier, and Margaret Maltby for their outstanding efforts in abstracting the data from Bureau case files.

James Brakora and Jack Miron of the Bureau of Workers' Disability Compensation contributed by trusting me enough to allow the effort to go forward, even though it did cause some administrative inconvenience. Karl Benghauser, Gary Calkins, and Jeff Knoll were extremely important to the study by serving both as sounding boards and sources of information.

Peter Barth once again gave the benefit of his wise counsel throughout the study. My colleagues at the Institute, Saul Blaustein, Wayne Wendling, Phyllis Buskirk, Jo Reece, and Phil Scherer, also assisted in various ways with the analysis or presentation of the ideas. My secretary, Irene Krabill, suffered with this manuscript more than anyone else. It has clogged her files for the last three years. Without her assistance I don't think I could have put all the bits and pieces together into one monograph. The rest of the Institute support staff did their usual excellent job. It is a genuine pleasure to work with them.

Last, I want to express my gratitude to the Director of the W. E. Upjohn Institute, the late Dr. E. Earl Wright. Earl brought me to Michigan to do research on workers' compensation. He pointed me toward Lansing and urged me to make whatever contribution I could. I thank Earl for the confidence he placed in me despite risk of political embarrassment. I thank Earl for getting me the resources I needed to do the job. And I thank Earl for providing an environment conducive to policy research. I truly cannot express how much I will miss his leadership.

CONTENTS

MICHIGAN CLOSED CASE SURVEY
ORIGINS and TECHNICAL DESCRIPTION

1

Introduction

This study was conceived in 1978 as an attempt to bridge the very serious information gap inhibiting discussion of workers' compensation reform in Michigan. While the issues were acknowledged to be intensely controversial, discussion of specific reform proposals was made even more difficult by the absence of an acceptable data base for analysis of workers' compensation issues in Michigan.

Unfortunately, the Michigan Department of Labor's Bureau of Workers' Disability Compensation had never developed this capability. This was due to a combination of budget stringency and the laissez-faire philosophy of the Michigan statute. Michigan relies primarily on the private parties involved in a workers' compensation case to look after their own interests. The Bureau does require reports from the employer or insurer at the time of the injury, when compensation begins, when compensation is terminated, and other significant dates. But aside from notifying the worker of the earnings reported by his or her employer (for calculating the weekly benefit level) and checking the accuracy of the benefit calculation, there is little agency involvement in the typical uncontested workers' compensation case in Michigan.

1

One result is that there are very few statistics available on the Michigan case population.[1] The Bureau of Workers' Disability Compensation publishes an annual report which summarizes the year's case activity (in one table); they also conduct a Pay Lag Study which measures the promptness of payment of benefits by individual carriers and self-insurers.[2] In addition, the Statistical Information Division of the Bureau of Safety and Regulation uses the Employer's Basic Report of Injury to analyze compensable accidents in Michigan.[3] But none of these efforts provides the information on durations of disability, weekly compensation amounts, or the other case details required for a well informed discussion of the impact of various reform proposals. It was an attempt to fill this gap that motivated the Michigan Closed Case Survey (MCCS).

For some purposes the MCCS has been successful in filling the gap, for others less so. It is fair to say that the workers' compensation system in Michigan proved much more complex than anticipated. In some cases, the system itself affects behavior so profoundly as to make it impossible to determine what is stimulus and what is response. This will be shown to be particularly vexing for the contested or litigated cases in Michigan. Since they are observed through the eyes of the official system itself, it is impossible to do more than repeat what is reported, with the appropriate caveats about the sources of the information.

Fortunately for the State of Michigan, the actual reform efforts quickly overtook the attempt to complete and publish this analysis. During the period of reform activity, from mid-1979 through late 1981, the data base described herein was repeatedly tapped for answers to questions which ranged from the prosaic to the arcane. Hopefully, the MCCS was a useful source of information in the process of overhauling Michigan's workers' compensation system; that, after all, was the major objective of the data collection effort.

To the extent this objective was achieved, the present volume describes a workers' compensation system that no longer exists. The amendments enacted in 1980 and 1981 have substantially altered Michigan's system.[4] Nevertheless, the publication of this volume was judged to be worthwhile. It provides a quantitative picture of the system in 1978, a point prior to any statutory changes. This may prove useful in assessing the impact of amendments to the statute. It also contributes in a minor way to filling the information gap about specific workers' compensation systems.

It is important not to promise too much, however. This volume does not constitute an introduction or guide to the Michigan workers' compensation system of 1978. It describes a data base derived from that system, but provides only a very imperfect reflection of the richness of detail present in the original.

This study also registers a substantial comment about the methodological difficulties of studying workers' compensation cases in general. It is submitted with the hope that someone else will find the inspiration to expand the frontiers of knowledge a little farther. If this can be accomplished, the Michigan Closed Case Survey and this description of it will be judged even more successful.

Sampling Design

The technical description of a sample is not very exciting, but it is very important. An understanding of the way in which the data were accumulated is crucial to comprehending the significance of particular results. This is especially true in the case of research on workers' compensation.

There is no standard accepted method of representing a workers' compensation case population. Because of the incredible variety of statutory provisions and administrative arrangements in state workers' compensation programs, there probably is no possibility of creating such a standard.[5] But owing to the significance of the issues and the lack of discussion of the alternatives elsewhere in the workers' compensation literature, the presentation of the empirical issues in this chapter is even more involved than usual.

This discussion is offered in the hope that it will contribute to an understanding of the conceptual difficulty of representing a dynamic workers' compensation population and the way in which the type of representation elected shapes the results. The reader who has little patience with such technical matters can omit this material. Where the sampling design has critical implications for the interpretation of empirical results later in the monograph, the problems raised here will be reiterated in terms that are directly relevant to the issue at hand.

A workers' compensation case population can be thought of in either static or dynamic terms, that is, either as a stock or a flow. On any given day there are a specific number of cases receiving weekly benefit payments, awaiting a hearing before an administrative law judge, pending appeal from a decision, or in any other status. It is theoretically possible to inventory the case population in any such state on any particular day and derive a measurement of this sub-population.

The Michigan Bureau of Workers' Disability Compensation conducts one such measurement of the stock of cases receiving weekly benefits as of December 31 each year. For each case in weekly benefit payment status, the employer is required to report the date of the injury, the insurer carrying liability for the injury, the weekly rate of compensation, the total amount of weekly compensation paid in the past calendar year to this individual, and the period for which such payments were made. This information is very useful for some purposes, but ultimately it is the underlying flow of workers' compensation cases through the system that is needed to assess what is happening in the program.

While it is interesting to know how many cases are in current payment status right now, it is more interesting to ask, How long have they been there? or, How long did it take to get there? or, What route did they follow to get there? or even, How long will they be there? Therefore, the essence of a workers' compensation case population is dynamic rather than static, a flow rather than a stock concept. The issue for the observer is how best to represent this dynamic population in a sample of cases for detailed analysis.

Since the population is dynamic, the sampling strategy must include a "slice-in-time" element; it is necessary to artificially interrupt the continuous flow of cases through the system to derive a sample. Thus the time signature of the cases from which a sample will be drawn must be carefully specified. Conceptually, there are three slice-in-time sampling designs that could be employed. One could accumulate a sample of cases (1) as they enter the system, (2) as they leave the system, or (3) somewhere in between. The bulk of the available statistics in Michigan have been based on the first approach.

The Employer's Basic Report of Injury (Form 100) must be filed for any occupational injury or disease involving seven or more lost workdays, or for a fatality, or any scheduled injury. It includes information about the injured employee, the nature and cause of the injury, and in addition identifies the employer and the insurance carrier. This form initiates a case in the Bureau of Workers' Disability Compensation files. It is subsequently coded for machine processing by the Injury Analysis Division of the Michigan Bureau of Safety and Regulation, which uses these data to study the pattern of industrial injury in Michigan in order to target safety education and inspection resources in an optimal manner. They also are reported to the U.S. Bureau of Labor Statistics' Supplementary Data System (SDS), a data bank providing comparable information on a number of states.[6]

This new SDS resource is expected to be valuable in guiding federal decisions about occupational safety and health policy as well.

The fundamental flaw in these data for describing the functioning of the Michigan workers' compensation system lies in the fact that only about three-fourths of the claims begin with a Form 100. In a great many cases there is no obvious accident implying worker disability and hence no reason for an employer to file Form 100. Many occupational disease disabilities, for instance, cannot be traced to a particular incident, identifiable as to time and place, but rather arise gradually over a period of time. The same would be true in situations where subsequent disability develops as a consequence of an incident that seemed relatively harmless at the time, as in infectious disease or even cumulative trauma cases.

Since these cases present the greatest evidentiary problems for workers' compensation, and frequently involve the most serious disabilities, an examination of compensation in only those cases that commence with Form 100 would be seriously flawed. This is confirmed by the fact that among the litigated workers' compensation cases in Michigan (those that involve an application for hearing), the MCCS reveals that two-thirds have *never* had a Form 100 filed.

There is an additional problem with a common case origin date as a sampling strategy, particularly in litigated cases. If a claim is contested, a hearing is scheduled. But it took an *average* of 468 days for disposition of a case by the Bureau's Hearings Division in 1978.[7] Thus, to get a relatively complete picture of the compensation experience for cases originating in one slice-in-time, it would be necessary to wait two or three years just to be sure that decisions are reasonably certain in contested cases. If one wanted to also observe a substantial period after resolution of the dispute to determine how the case was proceeding, even longer delays would be necessary.[8]

The problem is that workers' disabilities have continuous histories just like the workers, and to rush to judgment on the compensation system before the full consequences of an injury became apparent would be to bias the results in favor of the adequacy of the system. The really tough test comes in the difficult, involved cases that may take many years to draw to a conclusion. While these cases may not be very numerous, they are important to the social judgment of the efficacy of the workers' compensation system.

This difficulty is compounded by the necessity of working with public sector data. Insurance carriers have to make provision for future claims and for future developments in current claims well in advance; but they are not required to report reserves on individual claims, so these data are not available in the public sector.

To illustrate the problem, consider the experience of the insurance industry with the Michigan Special Call sponsored by the Michigan Workers' Compensation Rating and Inspection Association. They gathered data on a sample of claims filed in the months of March and October of 1976. Carriers were asked to evaluate these claims as of April 1, 1979, either two-and-one-half or three years after initiation. While only 4.3 percent of these claims were still open at the observation point, they accounted for 35 percent of the incurred indemnity costs.[9] These are clearly the most expensive cases; they may also be the most difficult cases to resolve. The performance of the workers' compensation system in these cases could not be reviewed with any sense of finality by anyone in 1979. Lacking information about reserves, all one could report is that these cases are still open.

Another sampling design which might be adopted would be a cross-section sample of all cases in the workers' compensation system at one point in time. This is the stock approach mentioned briefly earlier, a static representation of the case population flow at one "moment." Of course, all of these cases would be "unresolved" in the same sense as the difficult cases just discussed. One could not be sure what was *going* to happen in these cases; only what *was* happening at the time of the survey.

This second major conceptual approach is represented by the present Bureau of Workers' Disability Compensation Form 103, Annual Report on Payment of Compensation. These reports are to be filed by January 31 for each case being paid weekly benefits at the end of December of the preceding year. There are a given number of cases being compensated under the law at any point in time, and one might be interested in examining the compensation experience of these cases. This would be a relevant way to estimate the total weekly benefits being paid, for instance.[10]

However, this is not a useful approach to describing the performance of the system as a whole unless the stock of cases at a point in time can be related precisely to the underlying flow of cases through the system. This flow could be estimated for Michigan if Form 103 contained a complete retrospective compensation history, but since it is directed only at payments during the previous calendar year, it cannot yield accurate case population parameters.

There is also potential trouble with litigated cases under this design. It is not obvious when, or if, an insurer would file Form 103 in such a case. If a case is being contested, the insurer is generally not under any obligation to pay until and unless some resolution is reached. So it would not be expected that Form 103 would be filed while the case is being contested. On the other hand, once the dispute is resolved, the payments, if any, may also obviate the need for Form 103. Many of these cases are compromised and payment is made in a lump-sum which redeems the employer's liability forever, thereby closing the case. Form 103 would not be required in these cases either. Thus with this sampling design it would seem possible to reach only those contested cases where periodic benefits are eventually paid. Results to be reported later show that in Michigan this is only about 10 percent of all contested cases.

In addition, this design would impose severe problems in obtaining the sampling frame in the State of Michigan. There is no available listing of active cases, there are only active case files. It has been estimated that there are well over 100,000 workers' compensation cases active at any time, and it is not possible to freeze these files while a sample is drawn.[11] Thus there is little hope of obtaining a cross-section sample of all cases in the system in the straight cross-section sampling design.

We come finally to the closed case sampling design. In this instance, the sample consists of all cases *closed* in a given period of time. The chief strength of this approach lies in the fact that every case opened must be closed. Whether compensation is paid or not, whether the case is contested or not, regardless of the outcome, the case will eventually be closed. Sometimes closed cases will be reopened in the future as circumstances change, but a sample of cases closed during any particular period should also contain the appropriate number of these cases from earlier periods, so this factor could be measured as well.

The second advantage to a closed case design is that it minimizes uncertainty. The maximum amount of information is available about the case. Not only the probability of contention, but the fact of contention and its outcome will be known at closure. Not simply the compensation rate, but aggregate compensation paid over the life of the case is known at closure. Thus more and better information can be secured than with any other design.

The drawback is that this information may not be timely. To illustrate this problem, consider an accident occurring 20 years ago which led to permanent disability and which triggered the commencement of income maintenance and medical and rehabilitation benefits at that time. If there has been no substantive change in the circumstances of the disabled worker, benefits are still being paid (absent an agreement to redeem the employer's liability). Turning up such a case in a sample has the desirable aspect that it aids in establishing estimates of the actual population of such cases coming through the system; but it is doubtful that the compensation system of today bears close resemblance to the one of 20 years ago. Hence the compensation experience of this claimant cannot tell much about the performance of the current system.

The problem is that there are three reasons why a case may be old (i.e., many years since injury) at time of closure. The case may have been processed rapidly, compensation established without serious contention, and benefits paid for many years before recovery, or perhaps death, of the claimant. On the other hand, the case may have been littered with delays and contention for years, then finally redeemed with a lump-sum payment and it is all over in a matter of weeks. The third possibility is one where the disability is not manifest for some years and a claim is not entered until considerable time has passed, as in a latent occupational disease case. The closed case survey approach tolerates the first of these types, even though little useful information is gleaned from such cases, in order that the possibility of including the last two shall be maintained.

A closed case sample is representative of the underlying population, but, in a sense, it represents the workers' compensation case populations at the times the cases originated rather than at the time of closure. The 12-year-old disability cases that closed during the sample period represent not today's cases, but rather the cases of 12 years ago with a 12-year disability duration. Since the number of cases tends to grow through time, the less serious short duration cases are "representative" of a more recent (and generally larger) case population cohort than are the long duration cases. Therefore, the number of long duration cases in the sample understates the number of similar length disability cases in the current population, other things equal.

This problem, referred to by one insurance executive as the "small potatoes" effect, cannot be overcome with a closed case data base. If the case population is growing through time, a closed case sample will underestimate the incidence of long term disability claims, and overemphasize the short term, relatively routine cases. When one combines this underrepresentation of long term cases with the fact that these cases will not be representative of current policy by virtue of their distant origins, the closed case design is revealed to have significant failings as well.

Nevertheless, as a practical matter, a closed case design was judged to be preferable for the descriptive tasks that are the objective of this effort. It is the most workable sampling design, given the type of access to the population provided by the Michigan workers' compensation administrative system. No other claims will be made for the superiority of a closed case sampling design. Later in this chapter, however, the durations of disability from the MCCS will be compared to those from the Michigan Special Call to assess empirically the actual magnitude of the bias introduced.

MCCS Sampling Procedure

The Bureau of Workers' Disability Compensation case closure, or retirement, process was the focal point of the sampling design employed for this study. Since all workers' compensation claims, regardless of compensation status or litigation status, come through the case closure procedure in much the same way, it was the logical place to look for a handle on this dynamic case population.[12]

Case files at the Bureau of Workers' Disability Compensation are divided into uncontested (called "flats") and contested (called "folders") according to their administrative treatment. The flats generally consist simply of the Bureau forms reporting the injury itself (Form 100, Employer's Basic Report of Injury), the commencement of weekly compensation payments (Form 101, Notice of Commencement of Compensation Payments), and the termination of those payments (Form 102, Notice of Stopping of Compensation Payments). As mentioned earlier, the contested cases frequently do not have the Employer's Basic Report of Injury, but they do have Bureau Form 104, Petition for Hearing, which initiates a folder containing all the other papers attendant to a litigated claim. This paper trail can be quite voluminous in a case with a full hearing and transcript, or it can be minimal in a case that was redeemed without weekly compensation payments.

Active cases are maintained in a common file in alphabetical order according to the claimant's name. Upon retirement, or closure, the flats and folders are separated and accumulated in temporary storage space within the Bureau offices. As the temporary storage space is filled, the flats or folders are boxed and shipped to the state records center at another physical location. Litigated cases are shipped approximately once a month, unlitigated about three times a year.

The funneling of all cases through this closure procedure was judged to provide the most efficient way of accumulating the slice-in-time samples from the continuous flow of cases through the workers' compensation system. The separation of litigated and unlitigated cases at that point also facilitated different sampling ratios from the two populations. This was thought to be desirable because it was anticipated that there would be more variety within the litigated case population, and a higher sampling ratio for litigated cases would provide a more rational allocation of case abstracting resources.[13]

The litigated sampling frame was one shipment lot, litigated cases that were retired between October 9 and November 9, 1978. A sampling ratio of 0.50 was used within that lot to achieve a completed litigated sample of 1,224 cases for analysis. Since the closure period was exactly one month, the sampling ratio for the slice-in-time litigated sample relative to the annual flow of litigated cases would be 1 in 24.

The unlitigated sampling frame consisted of 3,085 flats retired from November 1 through November 7, 1978. This was a fairly large batch, as the average had been 1,667 closures per week up to November 1. It had been planned to sample every other case here too, but due to the unexpectedly large frame, a sampling ratio of 1 in 3 was employed. After elimination of the cases with no lost time (i.e., not compensable), this procedure yielded a completed sample of 954 unlitigated cases for analysis. This slice-in-time sample is estimated to represent a 1 in 86 sample of all compensated unlitigated workers' compensation cases closed in 1978 in the State of Michigan.[14]

A copy of the instruments used for data collection in the two samples is included as an appendix. It also contains the set of instructions given to the case abstractors, who were retired Bureau of Workers' Disability Compensation employees.[15] The instruments were oriented to Bureau forms and sought to collect most of the significant case elements that could be quantified.

Are the Samples Representative

Using the slice-in-time sampling ratios, it is possible to inflate the completed samples of the Michigan Closed Case Survey to represent the population. This estimate can then be compared to official figures from the Bureau on the 1978 case population to help assess the representativeness of the samples. Table 1-1 presents these results for the estimated population (MCCS) and the actual population (Bureau) by type of case.

There are a number of discrepancies between the two distributions. First, since the official total of "Voluntary Payment" cases is on the basis of cases *accepted* for pay-

Table 1-1
1978 Case Population Estimated
from the Michigan Closed Case Survey
Compared to Actual

Bureau of Workers' Disability Compensation*		Category	Michigan Closed Case Survey**	
Number	Percent		Number	Percent
74,885	69.6	Voluntary payments	77,572	72.5
20,324	18.9	Redemptions (contested and uncontested)	20,520	19.2
2,612	2.4	Judges' opinions (including stipulations)	1,800	1.7
1,366	1.3	Contested and accepted	1,416	1.3
8,356	7.8	Withdrawn or dismissed	5,640	5.3
107,543	100.0	Total	106,948	100.0

*As reported in *LABORegister,* July 1979, pp. 203-204. Voluntary payments are estimated on an accepted case basis. Other categories are actual counts of case determinations in 1978.

**Estimated 1978 closures based on samples of 954 unlitigated cases closed November 1 through November 7, 1978 and 1,224 litigated cases closed October 9 through November 9, 1978. Sampling ratios of 1 in 86 for the unlitigated sample and 1 in 24 for the litigated sample were used to inflate the sample to represent the entire 1978 closed case population. It should be noted that "closure" in the samples refers to the date the Bureau filed the cases for permanent storage, not the date the insurer closed the case.

ment, it would be expected to differ somewhat from the number of cases *closed* in a like period just because of the gradual expansion in the number of cases. The growth in the case population should bias the MCCS estimate upward as well, since the sample cases closed come from later in the year. Assuming the number of cases closed grows month by month, the true population for the entire year should be overestimated by a late-year sample. Table 1-1 shows that the number of voluntary payment cases is overestimated slightly by the MCCS.

A more serious sample problem revealed by table 1-1 is the deficit in "Judges' Opinions" and in the "Withdrawn or Dismissed" categories. While it is impossible to say for certain, this could be due to an unanticipated seasonality in litigated case closures. As reported earlier, the sample litigated cases were retired by the Bureau between October 9 and November 9, 1978. But the hearings for over three-fourths of these cases took place in July and August, prime vacation months. It may be that the number of hearings was lower than normal due to summer vacations.

The number of redemptions appears to be estimated closely by the samples, but the proportion is slightly higher due to the deficits in other categories. Given these various discrepancies, the very close estimation of the total workers' compensation case population for 1978 by the Michigan Closed Case Survey should not be taken too seriously. To some degree, it reflects the *ex post* method of calculating the sampling ratio for unlitigated cases, and to some degree it is a result of offsetting errors. There is no way to verify the representativeness of the samples within each case type due to the lack of any official data.

Tables 1-2 and 1-3 address the issue of representativeness of the insurers in the MCCS unlitigated sample. The Michigan Bureau of Workers' Disability Compensation conducts an annual Pay Lag Study on the routine cases that come through the administrative process. The time between notification of injury and issuance of first check is measured for each case. These distributions are reported for each authorized insurer in Michigan. The total number of cases listed for each insurer should approximate the number of compensable cases accepted voluntarily during 1978. This figure can be compared to the proportion of cases in the

Table 1-2
Insurance Carrier Representation - MCCS Unlitigated Sample

Insurance carriers	1978 BWDC pay lag study[a]		MCCS unlitigated	
	Cases	Percent	Cases	Percent
Michigan State Accident Fund................	4,013	9.1	48	8.4
Liberty Mutual	3,845	8.7	74	13.0
Michigan Mutual Liability	3,087	7.0	39	6.8
Travelers.................................	2,236	5.1	21	3.7
Aetna Casualty & Surety	1,984	4.5	34	6.0
Employers Mutual Liability of Wisconsin	1,916	4.3	27	4.7
Insurance of North America	1,749	4.0	20	3.5
Home Indemnity	1,721	3.9	20	3.5
Citizens of America........................	1,520	3.4	10	1.8
C.N.A.	1,384	3.1	16	2.8
Hartford Accident & Indemnity	1,345	3.0	16	2.8
Associated Indemnity	1,049	2.4	17	3.0
American Insurance Co......................	898	2.0	9	1.6
American Mutual Liability...................	745	1.7	8	1.4
Sentry	689	1.6	4	0.7
American Motorist	599	1.4	8	1.4
Auto Owners	588	1.3	10	1.8
Great American	582	1.3	8	1.4
Royal Indemnity & Royal Globe	521	1.2	2	0.4
National Union Fire of Hartford..............	517	1.2	11	1.9
Total 20 largest insurance carriers	30,988	70.1	402	70.4
All insurance companies...................	44,192	100.0	571	100.0
All cases (including self-insurers)	68,516		934	
Twenty largest insurance carriers as percent of all cases.....................	45.2%		43.0%	

a. Reported in *LABORegister,* July 1979, pp. 205-212.

Columns may not add to total due to rounding.

Table 1-3
Self-Insurer Representation - MCCS Unlitigated Sample

Self-Insurers	1978 BWDC pay lag study[a]		MCCS unlitigated	
	Cases	Percent	Cases	Percent
General Motors	4,732	19.5	74	20.4
Chrysler	2,170	8.9	30	8.3
Ford	1,289	5.3	19	5.2
City of Detroit	1,009	4.1	12	3.3
Michigan Hospital Association	407	1.7	7	1.9
Meijers Inc.	386	1.6	4	1.1
Bormans, Inc.	368	1.5	6	1.7
National Steel	338	1.4	16	4.4
Kresge S.S.	294	1.2	4	1.1
Kroger	281	1.2	3	0.8
Gulf & Western Ind. Inc.	242	1.0	1	0.3
Detroit Tooling Association	239	1.0	3	0.8
School Employers Group	238	1.0	2	0.6
Chatham Supermarket, Inc.	236	1.0	2	0.6
Michigan Municipal Fund	225	1.0	9	2.5
Detroit Board of Education	219	1.0	4	1.1
Keeler Brass	215	0.9	2	0.6
Sears Roebuck	208	0.9	2	0.6
Michigan Bell Telephone	206	0.8	1	0.3
Eaton Manufacturing Co.	203	0.8	1	0.3
Total 20 largest self-insurers	13,505	55.5	202	55.6
All self-insurers	24,324	100.0	363	100.0
All cases (including carriers)	68,516		934	
Twenty largest self-insurers as percent of all cases	19.7%		21.6%	

a. Reported in *LABORegister,* July 1979, pp. 205-212.

Columns may not add to total due to rounding.

MCCS unlitigated sample for each insurer as a rough test of the representativeness of the insurer distribution in the MCCS.

Table 1-2 presents this comparison for the 20 largest workers' compensation insurance carriers in Michigan, according to the 1978 Pay Lag Study. The MCCS figures are subject to sampling variability, especially since the slice-in-time sampling period was so short. However, the proportion of large carriers in the MCCS sample looks quite good, and the distribution among the 20 largest carriers appears satisfactory. Table 1-3 repeats this comparison, but for the 20 largest self-insurers reported in the 1978 Pay Lag Study. The results generally confirm the belief that the MCCS unlitigated sample adequately represents the self-insurer distribution in the population.

In summary, it appears from the very limited comparisons that can be made with the official statistics on the population of workers' compensation cases in Michigan, that the Michigan Closed Case Survey does represent that population fairly well. The proportions of various types of outcomes show some discrepancy, particularly those requiring a judge's opinion, but overall, the samples seem sound. As always when dealing with sample data, specific statistics are subject to sampling variability. Tests of significance will be reported in each table to reflect the influence of this factor.

The Closed Case Bias

As a rough check on the degree of distortion introduced by a closed case design, the disability duration distribution from the Michigan Closed Case Survey can be compared to that derived from the unpublished 1979 Michigan Special Call as analyzed by the National Council on Compensation Insurance. This was a special data collection effort sponsored by the Workers' Compensation Rating and Inspection Association of Michigan to provide input for the workers' compensation reform discussions in Michigan. The survey covered the 23 largest workers' compensation insurance carriers in Michigan, doing approximately 80 percent of the workers' compensation insurance business in the state. These carriers were asked to report as of April 1, 1979 the status of claims filed in the months of March and October of 1976, either two-and-a-half or three years earlier. In the conceptual terms employed here, this constitutes a slice-in-time sample based on the date of entry to the system.

The evaluation of the status of these cases must in some cases be based upon anticipation, since not all will have been finally resolved in two-and-a-half or three years. In fact, of the 5,355 claims sampled, 5,124 or 95.7 percent had been closed by the evaluation date of April 1, 1979. Data reported on the unresolved claims reflect the judgment of the claims processors in the various insurance companies as to the ultimate disposition of the case. While this is their profession, and the estimates are undoubtedly done as well as possible, they will not be precisely correct. Still, a comparison of results from the two different sampling strategies at roughly the same time is illuminating.

Table 1-4 compares the duration of disability distributions from the two data sources. It should be mentioned that the MCCS figures are for the insurance carrier segment of the workers' compensation case population; self-insurers are excluded. Cases are weighted so as to provide the correct proportion of litigated and unlitigated cases. In addition, the lump-sum settlements in the MCCS were given imputed durations of disability using the *average* weekly compensation rates for carrier cases observed in the samples rather than the claimant's specific weekly compensation rate. Given the restricted range of weekly compensation rates in Michigan, this should not introduce much bias, but it depends on the average date of injury. If the lump-sum cases are considerably older than the weekly benefit cases on the average, the imputed durations for these cases will be systematically biased downward. This is because their weekly compensation rate will be overestimated. The broad duration categories of table 1-4 should minimize such distortions, however.

The four columns of table 1-4 illustrate a number of points discussed earlier. The second column demonstrates the effect of truncating the sample at the two-and-a-half to three-year experience point. Since these cases were assessed either two-and-a-half or three years after claims were initially filed, among closed cases only lump-sum settlements could show more than three years duration. The other cases would not yet be closed. The effect is that only about one case in five anticipated to show a duration of over four years (as indicated by column 1) is actually counted in column 2. Column 2 shows a systematic bias with the degree of the bias varying directly with duration.

Column 3 shows the duration distribution of weekly payments for only those cases in the MCCS that were paid weekly compensation. It is quite similar to column 2, although the deficiency in the longest duration category is only about half as severe when compared to column 1. This column does not include any imputed durations for lump-sum cases, but does include all weekly payments made to those cases before settlement. Thus it represents only part of the compensation experience.

Table 1-4
Estimated Durations of Disability
for Michigan Workers' Compensation Cases

Duration of disability	NCCI Michigan special call		MCCS - carrier segment only	
	All cases (1)	Closed cases (2)	Weekly cases (3)	All cases (4)
Up to 26 weeks	88.9%	92.0%	92.3%	83.3%
26 to 52 weeks	4.6	4.3	3.1	6.2
1 year to 2 years	2.6	2.1	2.1	3.7
2 years to 4 years	1.9	1.1	1.5	4.0
Over 4 years	2.0	0.4	1.0	2.8
Total	100.0%	100.0%	100.0%	100.0%
	n=5,335	n=5,124	n=2,125 (weighted)	n=2,419 (weighted)

Columns may not add to total due to rounding.

The fourth column presents the distribution of durations in the MCCS, including imputed durations for lump-sum cases. It does not reveal the expected deficiency of long term cases; in fact, it seems to show an excess of such cases when compared to the NCCI distribution in the first column. Whereas the Michigan Special Call suggested that about 11 percent of compensable cases exceeded, or were expected to exceed, 26 weeks in duration of disability, the MCCS indicates nearly 17 percent had experienced this duration at closure. While these results must be taken as somewhat speculative, they certainly are interesting. In a direct interpretive sense, they mean that sampling variability may be greater than any systematic bias introduced by a closed case sampling design. Whether this conclusion would hold under other conditions is impossible to say.

In summary, the MCCS samples do not appear to have failed any of the tests of representativeness. There is a shortage of actual judges' decisions in the sample but, on the whole, the samples appear to represent the workers' compensation case population in Michigan fairly well. In addition, the theoretical bias introduced by a closed case design does not appear to be as serious in practice as anticipated, at least for the Michigan environment.

The data base has proved its viability in a technical sense. In chapter 2 it is used to describe Michigan's workers' compensation population in order to provide an empirical overview of the workers' compensation experience in Michigan. Chapter 3 focuses particularly on the litigation issue in the Michigan system. The correlates of litigation are explored and the outcomes are described in as much detail as is possible, given the quality of data available on litigated cases. Chapter 4 concentrates on indemnity benefit payments, reviewing both the adequacy and timeliness of indemnity payments in Michigan. The summary and conclusions of the study are presented in chapter 5.

NOTES

1. This is not just a Michigan failing. See Monroe Berkowitz and Stephen McConnell, "Uniform Data Systems and Related Subjects in Workers' Compensation," *Research Report of the Interdepartmental Workers' Compensation Task Force,* Volume 2 (Washington, DC: U.S. Government Printing Office, 1979), for a description of the general problem and a suggested solution.

2. These are published in the Michigan Department of Labor's monthly journal *LABORegister.* Annual reports of the Workers' Compensation Appeals Board and the Funds Administration are also published in this journal.

3. The results are published annually by the Michigan Department of Labor under the title *Compensable Injury and Illness Tabulations.* These data are used for diagnosing the nature of the safety problem and prioritizing areas for public attention.

4. Both sets of amendments have been briefly outlined in *LABORegister.* The changes introduced by the 1980 enactments were described in *LABORegister,* February 1981, pp. 28-30. The 1981 amendments were described in *LABORegister,* February 1982, pp. 22-23. There was also an overview of all the reforms in the Spring 1982 edition of *IAIABC Journal,* published by the International Association of Industrial Accident Boards and Commissions. See also H. Allan Hunt, "Reforms in Michigan's Workers' Compensation System," *Business Conditions in the Kalamazoo Area,* Second Quarter 1982, Vol. XXV, Number 2, pp. 19-23.

5. The most notable efforts to produce an overview of workers' compensation procedures are those of Monroe Berkowitz. See "The Processing of Workmen's Compensation Cases," Bureau of Labor Standards, Bulletin 310 (Washington, DC: U.S. Department of Labor, 1967). More recently, Monroe Berkowitz and John Burton reviewed ten state systems to determine the procedures and criteria used for permanent disability benefits. These results were reported as Part II of "Permanent Disability Benefits in the Workers' Compensation Program" (mimeo, October 1979), the final report to the National Science Foundation. An updated version of this study will be published by the W. E. Upjohn Institute for Employment Research in 1983.

6. See Norman Root and Michael Hoefer, "The First Work-Injury Data Available from New BLS Study," *Monthly Labor Review,* January 1979, pp. 76-80 and Norman Root and David McCaffrey, "Providing More Information on Work Injury and Illness," *Monthly Labor Review,* April 1978, pp. 16-21.

7. Bureau of Workers' Disability Compensation Annual Report, *LABORegister,* May 1979, p. 203.

8. It can safely be assumed that no policymaker would be willing to wait the additional two to three years for an appealed decision to be processed by the Workers' Compensation Appeal Board.

9. NCCI unpublished tabulations. Unfortunately, there is no published description of this valuable data base.

10. See H. Allan Hunt, *Inflation Protection for Workers' Compensation Claimants in Michigan: A Simulation Study* (Kalamazoo, MI: W. E. Up-john Institute for Employment Research, 1981), for an example of the way in which a dynamic element can be extracted from these static data.

11. At least it was not possible in 1978. The computerization of a case management data base may change this situation.

12. It is important to note that this description is of the process at the time of sampling in the Fall of 1978. It is not necessarily representative of current Bureau practice.

13. This turns out to have been insufficient to maximize the analytical potential of the sample. In retrospect, the sample should have been stratified by type of resolution but that was not appreciated at the time.

14. The sampling ratio was estimated by comparing the completed sample to official case management statistics. This differs considerably from the theoretical sampling ratio of 1 in 156 (one third of the cases from one week) due to the variability in the weekly case closure rate.

15. Thanks are due to Jo Walker of the Bureau staff for the suggestion that some former Bureau employees might be available for this work. It improved the quality of data immeasurably.

AN EMPIRICAL OVERVIEW
of WORKERS' COMPENSATION
in MICHIGAN

2

Introduction

It is very difficult to describe a workers' compensation system, regardless of the approach that is used. This is because of the number and diversity of cases and their specificity. Each case is special in that it represents an interruption, possibly a permanent disruption, in the normal routine of the injured worker. Each case is also unique, at least from the claimant's point of view. But because of the volume of workers' disability claims in Michigan, some generality is required to describe the workings of the compensation system overall.

Thus it is necessary to look for the broad trends and similarities among these diverse cases. While this leads to a perspective which tends to minimize the human aspects of these disability cases, it should not be taken to imply that the unique personal aspects of each disability claim are unimportant. Reaching a broader judgment of the facts does necessitate reducing the amount of detail retained on each observation. It is these details, however, that matter most to the injured worker and ultimately to the social judgment of the performance of the workers' compensation system.

As reported in chapter 1, the data for this study were abstracted from the official record of the case by people who knew what they were looking for. But one has only to read through a handful of the litigated case folders to see that the official record does not contain a very complete story. This problem is particularly acute for redemptions, where the record is very thin indeed. Even where a transcript of the hearing is available, it is difficult to assess the "facts" as presented in an intensely adversarial procedure. The most disappointing aspect is the medical expert testimony as to the nature and extent of the disability. Oftentimes it is hard to believe that the medical examinations put forward by the two sides were carried out on the same person.

This is not to be taken as a criticism of the administration of the workers' compensation system. Michigan's system was designed to be self-administering, with a relatively small, passive role for the state to play. But the effect is to leave the outside observer, dependent on official sources, with the task of trying to describe a very complex and bewildering array of disability cases with a sketchy and sometimes unreliable set of facts.

Nevertheless, this descriptive effort will concentrate on those facts. The attempt will be to present the numbers as they emerge from the Michigan Closed Case Survey—to try to construct an empirical description of workers' compensation in Michigan. For this purpose it is necessary to work with an integrated sample that combines the litigated and unlitigated samples described in chapter 1. Only by weighting the two samples appropriately can the entire workers' compensation system be addressed simultaneously.

Since unlitigated cases were sampled at a 1 in 86 rate and litigated cases were sampled at a 1 in 24 rate, the unlitigated cases will be inflated by a factor of 3.583 (86:24) to bring them into proper balance with the litigated. The integrated sample will therefore represent approximately one-half the number of cases closed in one month.[1] Thus in the presentation of weighted data to follow, there will be a maximum of 1,224 litigated cases and 3,418 unlitigated cases included. For hypothesis testing, the unweighted sample size will be used to avoid biasing the test statistics; but all tables will report weighted sample results. The reader should not be misled, however; the results reported here are based on the actual samples of 1,224 litigated and 954 unlitigated cases as reported in chapter 1.

The results of the data analysis will generally be reported separately for cases insured by workers' compensation insurance carriers and for the self-insured. The self-insured sector will be further divided into two groups: the big three automobile producers (General Motors, Ford, and Chrysler), and other self-insurers. This analytical treatment represents the most fundamental hypothesis of this study: that the Michigan workers' compensation experience is very different for these three insurer types. It also serves to highlight the major contribution of the MCCS over any other Michigan data base—the capability of comparing the insured sector to the self-insured.

In each table organized by insurer type, the chi-square statistic reported at the bottom of the tables gives the result of a test of the hypothesis that there are no differences between the three insurer types (the null hypothesis). The rejection of that hypothesis is indicated by the asterisk(s), with one asterisk indicating the hypothesis can be rejected at the 95 percent confidence level, two asterisks indicating the 99 percent confidence level. Thus the appearance of the asterisks after the chi-square statistic indicates that the differences among the insurer types in the sample are sufficient to reject the hypothesis that they are the same in the general case population. While this hypothesis may not always be the most critical, it provides a useful organizational device for the presentation. It should also help to remind the reader that these are sample data and are always subject to sampling variability. With these preliminary comments in place, the empirical description of the workers' compensation system in Michigan can proceed.

The Claims and the Claimants

The most fundamental administrative distinction among workers' compensation cases in Michigan is between litigated and unlitigated cases (also referred to as contested and uncontested). Table 2-1 shows that about one-fourth of Michigan's workers' compensation cases are litigated. Either the claimant or the employer can file a Petition for Hearing (Form 104), although when the employer files it is frequently called a "petition for determination of rights." This form initiates an administrative process whose major elements are: (1) serving a notice of dispute on the opposing parties and their counsels, (2) setting the case for pre-trial conference, and (3) a hearing of the dispute before an administrative law judge. Almost all of the petitions in Michigan are filed by claimants, nearly always with representation by an attorney.

Table 2-1 also reveals that the litigation rate among workers' compensation cases in Michigan is much higher for the automobile industry (big three) than for either the insured sector or other self-insured employers. Based on the MCCS, it appears that nearly half of the big three's workers' compensation cases are litigated. In contrast, only about one case in five is litigated by other insurers. The chi-square statistic shows that this difference is statistically very significant; that is, the difference among insurer types cannot be attributed to sampling variability alone (at a 99 percent level of confidence). The conclusion is that the litigated proportion does vary systematically across insurer types in Michigan. This phenomenon will be addressed more fully in the next chapter where the determinants of litigation will be probed.

Table 2-1
Type of Case by Insurer Type

| Type of case | Total | | Insurer type | | | | | |
| | | | Carrier | | Big three | | Other self-insurers | |
	Number	Percent	Number	Percent	Number	Percent	Number	Percent
Unlitigated	3,347	73.9	2,046	77.9	437	52.3	864	81.0
Litigated	1,179	26.1	579	22.1	398	47.7	202	19.0
Total	4,526	100.0	2,625	100.0	835	100.0	1,066	100.0
Missing cases	117							
Grand total	4,642							

Chi-square (unweighted) = 121.23** with 2 degrees of freedom.

Unlitigated cases are inflated by a factor of 3.583 to compensate for the smaller sampling ratio in the unlitigated sample.

Columns may not add to total due to rounding.

As interesting as the fact of litigation is the method of resolution of workers' disability claims in Michigan. Table 2-2 shows that an estimated 18 percent of all Michigan workers' compensation cases are settled with a "redemption" of liability, more widely known as a compromise and release settlement. While the name redemption seems to be unique to the State of Michigan, the form of the agreement is not. It is a standard compromise and release in which the claimant agrees, in exchange for some consideration, to sign a release in favor of the defendant. In Michigan parlance, the insurer "redeems" his or her liability for the disability in exchange for a negotiated cash payment.

It is important to understand that this agreement, after cursory review by an administrative law judge, amounts to a permanent release of liability for the injuries specified. The claimant is relinquishing any future claim, not only for income maintenance, but also for medical or rehabilitative treatment that may be required as a consequence of the accident or illness. This is the reason why some states have chosen to forbid this form of agreement. Such a prohibition does not reflect a judgment that the attorneys cannot adequately bargain for their clients. Rather, it is a statement that no one can foresee the ultimate consequences of an occupational injury or illness, and that under these circumstances there is justification for denying the parties the right to enter into such an agreement.

Analysis by insurer type reveals that the proportion of redemptions is more than twice as high among the big three auto producers, with approximately one-third of all their cases redeemed. Carriers redeem just under 16 percent and self-insurers other than the big three about 13 percent of their workers' compensation cases. Once again, the chi-square statistic indicates that the sample evidence is strong enough to conclude that the method of resolution does vary systematically by insurer type.

Table 2-2
Method of Resolution by Insurer Type

| Resolution | Total | | Insurer type | | | | | |
| | | | Carrier | | Big three | | Other self-insurers | |
	Number	Percent	Number	Percent	Number	Percent	Number	Percent
Redeemed	836	18.5	412	15.7	284	34.0	140	13.1
Withdrawn	261	5.8	167	6.4	54	6.4	41	3.8
Dismissed	59	1.3	23	0.9	28	3.4	8	0.8
Accepted	59	1.3	34	1.3	13	1.6	12	1.1
Decision	71	1.6	36	1.4	23	2.8	12	1.1
Voluntary	3,239	71.6	1,953	74.4	434	51.9	853	80.0
Total	4,526	100.0	2,625	100.0	835	100.0	1,066	100.0
Missing cases	117							
Grand total	4,642							

Chi-square (unweighted) = 116.14** with 10 degrees of freedom.

Unlitigated cases are inflated by a factor of 3.583 to compensate for the smaller sampling ratio in the unlitigated sample.

Columns may not add to total due to rounding.

Another category of resolution in table 2-2 is the proportion of cases withdrawn before the scheduled hearing. Generally this means the petition was *withdrawn without prejudice,* i.e., it can be filed again in the future. The *dismissed* category refers to cases that the administrative law judge finds unworthy; usually they are dismissed for lack of prosecution by the applicant. The *accepted* cases are those that the employer or carrier accepts "voluntarily" after a request for hearing but before the dispute has been fully adjudicated. In other words, something that arises in the course of litigation persuades the insurer that the claim is worthy after all.

The next category represents the actual *decisions* by the administrative law judge. These are in addition to the *proforma* approval of redemption agreements which constitute the other significant burden on the hearings process. For purposes of the analysis here, the decision category includes both those where benefits were awarded and where they were denied. Based on this closed case sample, formal decisions are required in less than 2 percent of all Michigan workers' compensation cases.

The final category in table 2-2 is for the cases paid voluntarily by the insurer. It represents the unlitigated majority of the workers' compensation case population. The variations in the proportion of cases paid voluntarily reflect the likelihood of litigation as presented in table 2-1. Since the big three experience the highest proportion of litigated cases, they are shown in table 2-2 with the lowest proportion of claims paid voluntarily.

Table 2-3 shows the geographic origins of workers' compensation cases in the MCCS broken down by insurer type. The sample is not large enough to estimate these proportions very precisely, but it is noteworthy that almost 55 percent of the workers' compensation cases in Michigan originate in the

Table 2-3
Geographical Location of Injury by Insurer Type

SMSA of injury	Total		Carrier		Insurer type Big three		Other self-insurers	
	Number	Percent	Number	Percent	Number	Percent	Number	Percent
Ann Arbor-Ypsilanti	141	3.4	84	3.6	37	4.6	20	2.0
Battle Creek	56	1.3	40	1.7	0	0	16	1.6
Detroit	2,281	54.8	1,135	48.0	530	65.1	617	62.6
Flint	246	5.9	66	2.8	151	18.6	29	3.0
Grand Rapids	338	8.1	265	11.2	0	0	73	7.4
Jackson	64	1.5	50	2.1	0	0	14	1.5
Kalamazoo-Portage	113	2.7	71	3.0	5	0.6	37	3.7
Lansing-East Lansing	151	3.6	71	3.0	30	3.7	50	5.1
Muskegon	94	2.3	83	3.5	0	0	12	1.2
Saginaw	108	2.6	46	2.0	54	6.6	8	0.8
Other areas	570	13.7	454	19.2	7	0.8	109	11.1
Total	4,163	100.0	2,365	100.0	813	100.0	985	100.0
Missing cases	480							
Grand total	4,642							

Chi-square (unweighted) = 348.61** with 20 degrees of freedom.
Unlitigated cases are inflated by a factor of 3.583 to compensate for the smaller sampling ratio in the unlitigated sample.
Columns may not add to total due to rounding.

Detroit SMSA. Nearly two-thirds of the self-insured cases come from Detroit. Detroit's employment in 1978 was 48 percent of the State of Michigan as a whole, so Detroit is somewhat overrepresented in the workers' compensation system.

Tables 2-4 and 2-5 show the nature of the injury and the injured part of the body, respectively, for closed Michigan workers' compensation cases. These data were coded according to the American National Standards Institute Z-16 standard and then collapsed into larger groupings for tabular presentations. The most common type of injury is the sprain or strain, with nearly 40 percent of all cases falling into this group. The large representation of multiple injuries and multiple body parts in the tables reflects the influence of the litigation procedure. When applicants file petitions for hearings, they or their attorneys frequently list multiple injuries. In fact, sometimes the petition reads like an index to the parts of the body. This inclusive approach to definition of injury is presumably helpful to the claimant during the litigation process, but it makes a realistic description of the injury very difficult in these cases.[2]

During the data collection for the MCCS, coders were instructed to record up to three specific injuries, particularly if they showed different injury dates. For analytical purposes, however, it seemed preferable to code such cases simply as multiple injuries. It should be pointed out that the result may not accurately represent the true nature of the injury. But there is no alternative to viewing these claims through the veil of the litigation process itself. Thus any distortions are introduced by the litigation process, not the reporting of the data *per se*.

This problem is also reflected in the comparisons among insurer types in nature of injury and part of body injured. The differences in proportions by insurer type seem to be a

Table 2-4
Nature of Injury by Insurer Type

Selected ANSI injury categories	Total		Insurer type					
			Carrier		Big three		Other self-insurers	
	Number	Percent	Number	Percent	Number	Percent	Number	Percent
Amputation	44	1.0	15	0.6	18	2.2	12	1.1
Burn	100	2.2	74	2.8	7	0.9	19	1.8
Bruise	548	12.2	319	12.2	104	12.5	125	11.8
Cut	420	9.3	264	10.1	61	7.4	94	8.9
Dislocation	62	1.4	42	1.6	6	0.7	14	1.3
Fracture	451	10.0	280	10.7	74	8.9	97	9.2
Hernia	154	3.4	108	4.1	21	2.5	25	2.4
Inflammation of joints	100	2.2	56	2.1	16	1.9	28	2.7
Sprain or strain	1,734	38.5	1,041	39.9	224	27.0	469	44.3
Multiple injuries	526	11.7	201	7.7	227	27.3	97	9.2
Other	293	6.5	167	6.4	65	7.9	61	5.7
Unclassified	69	1.5	44	1.7	8	1.0	17	1.6
Total	4,501	100.0	2,611	100.0	831	100.0	1,059	100.0
Missing cases	141							
Grand total	4,642							

Chi-square (unweighted) = 146.28** with 22 degrees of freedom.
Unlitigated cases are inflated by a factor of 3.583 to compensate for the smaller sampling ratio in the unlitigated sample.
Columns may not add to total due to rounding.

Table 2-5
Injured Part of Body by Insurer Type

Part of body	Total		Carrier		Insurer type Big three		Other self-insurers	
	Number	Percent	Number	Percent	Number	Percent	Number	Percent
Head or neck	152	3.4	99	3.8	20	2.4	34	3.2
Arm or wrist	306	6.8	182	7.0	55	6.6	68	6.4
Hand or finger	694	15.4	393	15.1	116	14.0	185	17.4
Abdomen	217	4.8	134	5.1	40	4.8	43	4.0
Back	1,005	22.3	603	23.1	117	14.1	285	26.8
Other trunk	242	5.4	159	6.1	24	3.0	58	5.5
Leg or ankle	573	12.7	362	13.9	81	9.8	129	12.2
Foot or toe	256	5.7	167	6.4	45	5.4	44	4.1
Multiple parts	855	19.0	392	15.0	282	34.0	181	17.0
Body system	160	3.6	83	3.2	45	5.4	32	3.0
Other	43	1.0	36	1.4	4	0.5	3	0.3
Total	4,504	100.0	2,611	100.0	830	100.0	1,063	100.0
Missing cases	138							
Grand total	4,642							

Chi-square (unweighted) = 102.22** with 20 degrees of freedom.
Unlitigated cases are inflated by a factor of 3.583 to compensate for the smaller sampling ratio in the unlitigated sample.
Columns may not add to total due to rounding.

consequence primarily of the number reporting multiple injuries. This in turn is a function largely of the proportion of all cases that are litigated. So while the chi-square statistic shows that the distribution of injuries does differ systematically by insurer type, this does not appear to be an important result analytically.

Table 2-6 shows the level of disability reported for weekly benefit cases by insurer type in Michigan. The bulk of claims are for temporary total disabilities. The overwhelming majority of these involve only one spell (or period) of disability. However, there are a significant number of cases reporting multiple spells. If the multiple total disability spells are combined with the total disability followed by a partial disability group, the sample indicates that about 5 percent of all Michigan cases do involve more than one period of weekly disability compensation payments.

It should be pointed out that this tabulation is oriented very strongly to the receipt of *weekly* benefits. This is illustrated by the other major category in table 2-6, "no weekly compensation." This group includes uncompensated cases, of course, but it is dominated by redemptions. Most of these never received any weekly indemnity payments at all; they are simply lump-sum settlements of disputed cases.

This reflects the practice in Michigan, but it also complicates the description of Michigan's disability cases in terms of the traditional disability categories. Michigan statute does not distinguish between temporary and permanent disabilities (except for defining "total and permanent disability" as a special group). Thus there is no need to certify the expected duration (or severity) of disability when a case is redeemed. All that appears in the record is a disputed allegation of a work-related disability, some contradictory medical testimony as to the condition of the claimant, and a lump-sum payment. The true nature and extent of disability

Table 2-6
Level of Disability by Insurer Type

Disability level	Total		Insurer type					
			Carrier		Big three		Other self-insurers	
	Number	Percent	Number	Percent	Number	Percent	Number	Percent
Total disability - one spell	3,180	70.4	1,969	75.2	401	48.1	810	76.1
Total disability - multiple spells	193	4.3	95	3.6	37	4.5	60	5.7
Total and partial disability	35	0.8	16	0.6	11	1.3	9	0.9
Partial disability	24	0.5	18	0.7	1	0.1	6	0.5
Scheduled loss	50	1.1	24	0.9	18	2.2	8	0.8
Fatality	5	0.1	1	0	4	0.4	0	0
No weekly compensation	1,030	22.8	496	19.0	362	43.5	171	16.1
Total	4,517	100.0	2,619	100.0	833	100.0	1,065	100.0
Missing cases	125							
Grand total	4,642							

Chi-square (unweighted) = 141.80** with 12 degrees of freedom.
Unlitigated cases are inflated by a factor of 3.583 to compensate for the smaller sampling ratio in the unlitigated sample.
Columns may not add to total due to rounding.

is generally not apparent. For this reason, table 2-6 is not comparable to an outwardly similar tabulation for other states.

It does introduce a fundamental distinction between weekly indemnity payments and lump-sum payments which will be maintained throughout this volume, however. Because of the confusion over what is a permanent and what a temporary disability, it seems preferable in a Michigan context to focus on the form of indemnity payment rather than the duration of disability.[3] This will occasionally produce some confusing results. For instance, table 2-6 indicates that only 0.1 percent of closed cases are fatalities. But this really means that 0.1 percent of closed cases were paid *weekly* survivor's benefits. Excluded from this figure is a much larger group of fatality claims that were redeemed and, hence, included in the no weekly compensation classification. Similarly for the partial disability category in table 2-6, only those cases that were paid partial weekly benefits under the wage-loss principle are included. Other partial disabilities that were redeemed are included in the no weekly compensation category.

The distortions resulting from these unusual factors in Michigan have been very troublesome in a number of ways. The National Council on Compensation Insurance, in analyzing Michigan loss data, groups together all permanent injuries that are not totally disabling, all temporary total disabilities with a duration in excess of one year, and lump-sum settlements of all cases other than permanent total disabilities. They call this amalgam "other permanent disabilities," and find that about 60 percent of indemnity losses arise from this category. It is clear that these are very different types of cases from a policy perspective, however, and it causes considerable confusion to lump them together. Whether the attempt to separate weekly payments and lump-sum payments, as done here, will prove more successful remains to be seen. It does provide an alternative way of looking at Michigan workers' compensation cases.

Continuing with the emphasis on weekly benefit payments, table 2-7 shows the reason the insurer reported for the termination of weekly benefits. Obviously, this table only includes closed cases that received some weekly benefit payments. Those cases that were redeemed without any weekly payments are represented among the missing cases in table 2-7. The message of this table is that the overwhelming majority of weekly payment cases in Michigan, nearly 90 percent, culminate in the claimant's return to work. This is as it should be, since a recovery from disability and return to work is always the primary goal of workers' compensation.

Turning to the characteristics of the claimants, table 2-8 indicates that about one-fourth of the workers' compensation claimants in Michigan are female, with a slightly lower proportion for the big three auto producers. Table 2-9 shows the age distribution of claimants by insurer categories. The most noteworthy features of this table are the elevated proportion of claims from older workers at the big three and the higher proportion of young workers in the insured sector. The former reflects the high incidence of litigated claims from auto industry retirees while the latter presumably reflects the younger workforce associated with smaller employers in the insured sector. Note that while the proportion of workers under 21 is twice as high for the carrier sector, the average age of claimants is not much different than that for other self-insurers. The big three claimants, on the other hand, do have a noticeably higher average age, 41 years compared to just over 36 for the carrier sector.

These differences are also reflected in tables 2-10 and 2-11, which show the reported number of dependents and average weekly earnings, respectively, by insurer type. According to table 2-10, about one-third of workers' compensation claimants in Michigan have no dependents. Furthermore,

Table 2-7
Reason Payments Stopped by Insurer Type

| Reason | Total | | Insurer type | | | | | |
| | | | Carrier | | Big three | | Other self-insurers | |
	Number	Percent	Number	Percent	Number	Percent	Number	Percent
Return to work	3,091	87.7	1,822	84.9	428	89.7	841	93.0
Dispute	7	0.2	7	0.3	0	0	0	0
Doctor's report	27	0.8	26	1.2	0	0	1	0.1
Benefit expired	29	0.8	17	0.8	7	1.5	5	0.5
Recovered	58	1.6	40	1.9	6	1.3	12	1.3
Redeemed	41	1.2	30	1.4	5	1.0	6	0.7
Other	273	7.7	203	9.5	31	6.5	39	4.3
Total	3,526	100.0	2,145	100.0	478	100.0	904	100.0
Missing cases	1,117							
Grand total	4,642							

Chi-square (unweighted) = 25.65* with 12 degrees of freedom.
Unlitigated cases are inflated by a factor of 3.583 to compensate for the smaller sampling ratio in the unlitigated sample.
Columns may not add to total due to rounding.

Table 2-8
Gender by Insurer Type

| Gender | Total | | Insurer type | | | | | |
| | | | Carrier | | Big three | | Other self-insurers | |
	Number	Percent	Number	Percent	Number	Percent	Number	Percent
Male	3,474	76.9	1,980	75.5	712	85.5	783	73.5
Female	1,045	23.1	641	24.5	120	14.5	283	26.5
Total	4,519	100.0	2,621	100.0	832	100.0	1,066	100.0
Missing cases	124							
Grand total	4,642							

Chi-square (unweighted) = 20.94** with 2 degrees of freedom.
Unlitigated cases are inflated by a factor of 3.583 to compensate for the smaller sampling ratio in the unlitigated sample.
Columns may not add to total due to rounding.

Table 2.9
Age at Injury by Insurer Type

Age	Total		Insurer type					
			Carrier		Big three		Other self-insurers	
	Number	Percent	Number	Percent	Number	Percent	Number	Percent
Through 20	404	10.1	295	13.0	45	6.1	65	6.6
21 to 30	1,176	29.4	689	30.3	194	26.2	293	29.7
31 to 40	847	21.2	448	19.7	138	18.7	261	26.5
41 to 50	553	16.3	381	16.7	128	17.3	145	14.7
51 to 60	540	16.0	316	13.9	147	19.9	177	18.0
Over 60	279	7.0	145	6.4	88	11.9	45	4.6
Total	3,999	100.0	2,274	100.0	739	100.0	986	100.0
			$\bar{X} = 36.4$		$\bar{X} = 41.0$		$\bar{X} = 37.6$	
Missing cases	543							
Grand total	4,542							

Chi-square (unweighted) = 54.45** with 10 degrees of freedom.
Unlitigated cases are inflated by a factor of 3.583 to compensate for the smaller sampling ratio in the unlitigated sample.
Columns may not add to total due to rounding.

Table 2-10
Number of Dependents by Insurer Type

| Dependents | Total | | Insurer type | | | | | |
| | | | Carrier | | Big three | | Other self-insurers | |
	Number	Percent	Number	Percent	Number	Percent	Number	Percent
None	1,554	34.9	1,036	40.0	184	22.7	334	31.9
One	1,144	25.7	570	22.0	281	34.7	293	28.0
Two	569	12.8	289	11.2	121	15.0	159	15.2
Three	534	12.0	311	12.0	97	12.0	126	12.0
Four	283	6.4	155	6.0	70	8.7	58	5.5
Five	143	3.2	81	3.1	25	3.1	37	3.6
Six	47	1.1	16	0.6	18	2.3	13	1.2
Seven or more	172	3.9	131	5.1	13	1.6	28	2.7
Total	4,447	100.0	2,590	100.0	810	100.0	1,047	100.0
			$\bar{X} = 1.6$		$\bar{X} = 1.8$		$\bar{X} = 1.6$	
Missing cases	196							
Grand total	4,642							

Chi-square (unweighted) = 75.25** with 14 degrees of freedom.

Unlitigated cases are inflated by a factor of 3.583 to compensate for the smaller sampling ratio in the unlitigated sample.

Columns may not add to total due to rounding.

Table 2-11
Weekly Earnings by Insurer Type

Weekly earnings categories	Total		Insurer type					
			Carrier		Big three		Other self-insurers	
	Number	Percent	Number	Percent	Number	Percent	Number	Percent
To $100	210	5.0	193	8.0	1	0.1	16	1.6
$101 - $200	1,207	29.0	894	36.9	74	9.9	238	24.1
$201 - $300	1,554	37.3	772	31.8	350	46.5	432	43.7
$301 - $400	779	18.7	326	13.5	258	34.2	195	19.8
$401 - $500	283	6.8	170	7.0	40	5.3	74	7.5
Over $500	132	3.2	69	2.8	30	3.9	33	3.4
Total	4,166	100.0	2,425	100.0	753	100.0	988	100.0
			$\bar{X} = \$235.71$		$\bar{X} = \$302.95$		$\bar{X} = \$272.09$	
Missing cases	477							
Grand total	4,642							

Chi-square (unweighted) = 207.21** with 10 degrees of freedom.

Unlitigated cases are inflated by a factor of 3.583 to compensate for the smaller sampling ratio in the unlitigated sample.

Columns may not add to total due to rounding.

this proportion varies substantially by insurer type with slightly over 20 percent of big three cases, 30 percent of other self-insurer cases, and 40 percent of carrier cases reporting no dependents. It is difficult to say how accurate this information may be, but these proportions do seem high. The number of dependents is reported by the claimant for litigated cases on the Petition for Hearing. However, if the case ends up being redeemed there is not likely to be any review of the number of dependents since it does not figure directly in the settlement. For cases that receive weekly compensation payments, the insurer reports the number of dependents, together with the average weekly wage and the calculated weekly benefit, on the form that notifies the Bureau of the commencement of weekly payments. The Bureau, in turn, notifies the disabled employee of this information and urges the worker to advise if it is incorrect.

This would seem to give the claimant an incentive to make sure the number of dependents is accurate. However, it is always possible that it is not taken seriously; or that some unknown reporting bias slips in. In particular, it could be that the employer reports the number of dependents claimed for tax withholding purposes, which could systematically understate the actual number. If the worker is not eligible for the maximum benefit, or is not well-informed on how benefit levels are figured, it is likely that no correction would be forthcoming.

Similar distortions could be present in table 2-11, weekly earnings by insurer type, since these data were gathered from the same sources. The average reported weekly wage for the entire sample was $256.49. But this measurement is for cases *closed* in 1978. The weekly earnings reported pertain to the time of the injury or origin of the case, not to the time of closure. Thus the wages reported in the MCCS do not represent one point in time, but a complex mixture of recent wages and older wages, according to the length of time the cases have been in the workers' compensation system.

Nevertheless, it is apparent from table 2-11 that there are very substantial differences in wage levels between insurer types in Michigan. A high proportion of injured low-wage workers are in the carrier insured sector. While 45 percent of the carrier sector claimants earned less than $200 weekly before being disabled, this was true for only 10 percent of the big three and 25 percent of other self-insurers' claimants. About 10 percent of claimants from each insurer type earned over $400 per week before their injury. This is a very surprising level of similarity, given what is known about auto industry wage levels.

Michigan's statute provides a maximum benefit at two-thirds of the state average weekly wage at the time of the injury; less if full dependency allowances are not claimed. So there is little incentive to accurately report earnings if they are greater than the state average weekly wage. The benefit formula would prevent recovery of such amounts anyway. Thus it is probable that the wages of high-earnings level claimants are systematically understated. For instance, the big three claimants are reported in table 2-11 as having earnings that are 18 percent more than the average for the whole sample. According to published figures, the weekly earnings of workers covered by unemployment insurance in the transportation equipment industry were about 58 percent higher than the statewide average in 1977.[4] The MCCS results would be biased downward by the incidence of litigation delays, long duration disabilities, retiree claims, and other influences; but the differential still appears unreasonably small. It is probably safe to conclude that the differences in average earnings in table 2-11 are significantly understated.

Compensation Payments[5]

These wage differences are also reflected in table 2-12, which shows the weekly compensation rate by insurer type. The extent of wage loss (total or partial) and the number of dependents also affect the weekly compensation payment, but it is primarily a function of the level of earnings. Table 2-12 shows that two-thirds of the cases closed in October and November of 1978 had received weekly payments between $100 and $150. A substantial minority of 25 percent received payments of over $150 per week and a small number received less than $100 weekly (about 9 percent). The differences among insurer types are substantial and statistically significant. This is true even though the distribution of weekly compensation rates is truncated at both ends by the maximum and minimum benefit levels.[6]

Table 2-13 demonstrates the actual significance of the minimum and maximum benefit levels in Michigan. Almost 64 percent of all weekly payment cases received the maximum benefit for their injury year and dependency classification; virtually every case for the big three employees. At the other end of the scale, about 15 percent of all closed weekly compensation cases received the minimum benefit. Reflecting the wage distribution results presented earlier, the bulk of these minimum benefit cases occur in the carrier sector.

Only one case in five actually received the statutory two-thirds of gross weekly earnings as the weekly benefit payment. It should perhaps be pointed out that this result is not affected substantially by the litigation process, nor by the incidence of lump-sum payments. These measurements pertain only to the cases that actually received weekly payments and refer to the maxima and minima in effect at that time. It is clear from this evidence that large wage level differences, filtered through a benefit structure which severely restricts

Table 2-12
Weekly Compensation Rate by Insurer Type

| | | | | | Insurer type | | | | |
| | Total | | Carrier | | Big three | | Other self-insurers | |
Compensation rate	Number	Percent	Number	Percent	Number	Percent	Number	Percent
$1 - $50	102	2.9	91	4.2	3	0.6	8	0.9
$51 - $100	210	5.9	137	6.4	31	6.5	42	4.6
$101 - $150	2,333	66.0	1,487	69.3	243	50.8	603	66.1
$151 - $200	892	25.2	432	20.1	201	42.0	259	28.4
Total	3,537	100.0	2,147	100.0	478	100.0	912	100.0
			$\bar{X}=\$127.32$		$\bar{X}=\$144.21$		$\bar{X}=\$138.60$	
Missing cases	1,106							
Grand total	4,642							

Chi-square (unweighted) = 64.60** with 6 degrees of freedom.
Unlitigated cases are inflated by a factor of 3.583 to compensate for the smaller sampling ratio in the unlitigated sample.
Columns may not add to total due to rounding.

Table 2-13
Benefit Rate by Insurer Type

Benefit rate	Total		Insurer type					
			Carrier		Big three		Other self-insurers	
	Number	Percent	Number	Percent	Number	Percent	Number	Percent
Minimum benefit	546	15.6	467	21.9	0	0	79	8.8
Two-thirds of wage	719	20.5	551	25.9	8	1.7	160	17.7
Maximum benefit	2,244	63.9	1,110	52.2	470	98.3	664	73.5
Total	3,509	100.0	2,127	100.0	478	100.0	904	100.0
Missing cases	1,134							
Grand total	4,642							

Chi-square (unweighted) = 197.07** with 4 degrees of freedom.

Unlitigated cases are inflated by a factor of 3.583 to compensate for the smaller sampling ratio in the unlitigated sample.

Columns may not add to total due to rounding.

the scope of the wage level in determining benefits, still produces widely varying weekly compensation experience.

This becomes very apparent when discussing possible legislative changes in the maximum and minimum benefit levels. Increasing the maximum benefit level would have a tremendous impact on the self-insured employers; much less on the insured sector. On the other hand, changes in minimum benefit levels would be of major concern to insured employers, and of little value to the self-insured. This was one of the reasons reform of the Michigan benefit formula was so difficult. The tradeoff among different provisions varied substantially by employer and/or insurer type.

It is time now to turn attention to the duration of disability issue. However, before presenting any data it is important to reiterate the bias, discussed in chapter 1, that is introduced with a closed case design. This potential bias is at its maximum when examining duration of disability. In the first place, the closed cases that involve long durations of disability represent an earlier, generally smaller case population. Thus they would tend to be outnumbered by short duration, more recent cases simply as a consequence of the growth of the labor force.

In addition, since lifetime benefits were only extended to the general disability category in Michigan in 1965, the case population may not yet be mature enough to have reached an equilibrium. This would lead to a further distortion in the number of long term cases relative to short term cases in a closed case survey. This concept can be explained with the aid of a few simplifying assumptions. Suppose it was possible to observe a workers' compensation system as it was going into operation for the first time. Suppose also that all cases with disability durations greater than one year would not close until exactly 10 years after the injury date. Assume that the same number of cases originate in each year. Any sample consisting of one month's *closed* cases drawn during the first ten years of system operation would not contain *any* long term cases, but would contain only cases with disability durations of less than one year. Thus a closed case sampling design would lead to the incorrect conclusions that there were *no* cases with disabilities lasting over one year.

Now, suppose instead of exactly a 10-year duration for long term disability cases, they were characterized by a distribution of durations. Assume that distribution was rectangular, so that the *average* duration of long term cases was 10 years, but they ranged from 1 year to 19 years with a constant number closing in each year. If a slice-in-time closed case sample was drawn in year two, a few long term cases would be represented, but they would be seriously underrepresented relative to the short term cases. This is because the long term cases would be from only one cohort. As time passes and the case population "matures" so that cases are closing from a number of earlier cohorts, the relationship between long term closures and short term closures would change substantially. This change is an artifact of the measurement technique, not a change in the underlying dynamics of case duration. Under the stated assumptions, it would take 20 years for the population to reach an equilibrium or steady state condition.

When this dynamic distortion phenomenon is imposed on a fluctuating case population with a very complex duration distribution, it becomes difficult even to describe the nature of the problem. However, it is a fact that a closed case survey tends to yield a distorted view of disability durations. It systematically underestimates the incidence of long duration disabilities. The magnitude of the error is a function of the frequency of long term cases and their duration distribution.

The empirical analysis of the closed case bias in chapter 1 showed that, for Michigan at least, this problem is not as big as it would seem. When the durations of disability from the MCCS were compared to those from another sample with a different sampling design, the closed case samples appeared to contain about one-third fewer cases with actual paid durations of one year or more. In chapter 1 it was shown that this was more than offset when the redemptions were given imputed durations based on the size of the lump-sum payments. These results should be treated with caution, however, by anyone whose focus is estimating the actual durations of disability as opposed to comparing the experience of different insurer types.

Table 2-14 shows a detailed distribution of compensation durations by insurer type. This table includes only the actual number of weeks paid; no lump-sum payments are included. The most striking feature of this table is the small number of cases with paid durations of one week to two weeks. This reflects the benefit waiting period provision in Michigan statute. Compensation for wage loss begins after one week of disability, but if the disability lasts two weeks or more, benefits are paid retroactively from the data of injury. The effect of this provision is that benefits are paid for either less than one week or more than two weeks, since the accumulation of one full week of compensated disability triggers payment for the first unpaid week as well.[7]

The other noteworthy element of table 2-14 is that the differences among the insurer types in the distribution of duration are *not* statistically significant. Even though the means are quite different, with a range of 10.1 weeks for other self-insurers to 16.7 weeks for the big three, the hypothesis that the distributions are the same cannot be rejected in this instance.[8] Because of this fact and because the sample numbers are very small, it is unwise to draw any conclusions about the apparent differences in the tails of the distribution for the three insurer types.

Table 2-14
Duration of Weekly Compensation Payments by Insurer Type

| Duration | Total | | Insurer type | | | | | |
| | | | Carrier | | Big three | | Other self-insurers | |
	Number	Percent	Number	Percent	Number	Percent	Number	Percent
Up to 1 week	741	21.1	493	23.2	84	17.6	163	17.9
1 to 2 weeks	234	6.7	140	6.6	40	8.4	54	5.9
2 to 4 weeks	860	24.5	502	23.6	122	25.5	236	26.0
4 to 8 weeks	776	22.1	456	21.5	99	20.7	220	24.2
8 to 13 weeks	336	9.6	210	9.9	42	8.7	84	9.2
13 to 26 weeks	290	8.3	158	7.5	44	9.3	87	9.6
26 to 52 weeks	123	3.5	66	3.1	21	4.4	36	4.0
1 to 2 years	73	2.1	44	2.1	11	2.3	18	2.0
2 to 4 years	44	1.2	33	1.5	5	1.0	6	0.7
Over 4 years	36	1.0	22	1.0	9	1.9	5	0.5
Total	3,513	100.0	2,125	100.0	479	100.0	910	100.0
			$\bar{X} = 12.3$		$\bar{X} = 16.7$		$\bar{X} = 10.1$	
Missing cases	1,129							
Grand total	4,642							

Chi-square (unweighted) = 17.00 with 18 degrees of freedom.
Unlitigated cases are inflated by a factor of 3.583 to compensate for the smaller sampling ratio in the unlitigated sample.
Columns may not add to total due to rounding.

The table does show the predominance of short duration disabilities in Michigan's workers' compensation system, however. Over 20 percent of the cases receiving periodic compensation payments are paid for one week or less. Over 50 percent of the cases involve no more than four weeks of disability. Furthermore, this experience holds for all insurer types. Even though the long duration cases are under-represented in table 2-14, this conclusion is firm since doubling the long duration cases would not change the overall distribution very much.

Table 2-15 shows the distribution of total weekly compensation paid by insurer type. It is closely related to table 2-14, since total weekly compensation is simply the product of the duration of benefits and the weekly compensation rate. The differences among insurer types in table 2-15 are statistically significant. This represents the contribution of the differences in weekly compensation rates reported in table 2-12. In this case, also, the major conclusion is that the system is dominated by small cases. Over 70 percent involve weekly indemnity of less than $1,000.

According to table 2-15, only about 3 percent of weekly payment cases show more than $8,000 in aggregate weekly indemnity. This number should be treated with some caution, however. Since the subject is weekly compensation payments only, the expensive cases are necessarily old cases with low weekly compensation rates (appropriate to earning levels at the time of the injury). Therefore, the realized cost of those cases is considerably less than a comparable duration case arising at the present time.

This whole discussion might be regarded as misleading by some, since all lump-sum payments have been omitted thus far. It was shown in table 2-2 that over 18 percent of Michigan's workers' compensation cases are redeemed, so discussing only weekly payment cases could introduce a very

Table 2-15
Total Weekly Compensation Paid by Insurer Type

Total weekly compensation	Total		Insurer type					
			Carrier		Big three		Other self-insurers	
	Number	Percent	Number	Percent	Number	Percent	Number	Percent
$1 - $125	752	21.2	505	23.5	81	16.9	166	18.2
$126 - $250	199	5.6	149	6.9	13	2.7	37	4.0
$251 - $500	822	23.2	484	22.5	123	25.8	215	23.7
$501 - $1,000	722	20.4	433	20.1	93	19.4	196	21.5
$1,001 - $2,000	548	15.5	303	14.1	85	17.7	161	17.7
$2,001 - $4,000	270	7.6	148	6.9	45	9.5	77	8.4
$4,001 - $8,000	125	3.5	62	2.9	22	4.6	41	4.5
$8,001 - $16,000	55	1.6	36	1.7	9	1.8	11	1.2
Over $16,000	48	1.3	33	1.5	8	1.7	7	0.8
Total	3,541	100.0	2,153	100.0	479	100.0	910	100.0
			$\bar{X} = \$1,372$		$\bar{X} = \$1,723$		$\bar{X} = \$1,237$	
Missing cases	1,101							
Grand total	4,642							

Chi-square (unweighted) = 26.52* with 16 degrees of freedom.
Unlitigated cases are inflated by a factor of 3.583 to compensate for the smaller sampling ratio in the unlitigated sample.
Columns may not add to total due to rounding.

serious bias. In fact, table 2-16 shows that the weekly payment cases and lump-sum payment cases can be treated as
separate populations. Less than 5 percent of all cases receive
both weekly and lump-sum indemnity payments. Nearly 74
percent of all closed cases received weekly indemnity
payments only, and about 15 percent received only lump-
sum payments. These proportions are somewhat similar for
the carrier sector and the other self-insured sector. The big
three auto manufacturers pay about three times as many
lump-sum cases relatively; but it is still true that there is very
little overlap with the weekly compensation cases.

Tables 2-17 and 2-18 address the other group of compensated cases: lump-sum payment cases. The vast majority of
these are redemptions, but there are a few scheduled loss
cases and lump-sum advance cases included as well. As indicated in table 2-16, 20 percent of the closed case sample
had received lump-sum payments. The cases receiving weekly compensation only and those receiving no indemnity at all
are counted as missing in tables 2-17 and 2-18.

Table 2-17 reports the size of gross lump-sums, whereas
table 2-18 covers net lump-sums. The difference between the
two is made up of the costs of litigation: namely, attorney's
fees, other legal costs, and medical costs. This issue will be
examined in chapter 4, but for now it is sufficient to point
out that the gross lump-sum is what the insurer pays and the
net lump-sum is what the claimant actually receives. Thus
when talking about the cost of lump-sum cases, it is appropriate to use the gross amount, but when discussing questions of benefit levels, net lump-sums are more appropriate.
The major focus here is on table 2-17, i.e., gross lump-sum
payment amounts.

The distribution of lump-sums is not at all similar to the
distribution of weekly payments. There are relatively few
small lump-sum payments, only 5 percent are under $1,000.

Table 2-16
Type of Compensation by Insurer Type

Compensation type	Total		Insurer type					
			Carrier		Big three		Other self-insurers	
	Number	Percent	Number	Percent	Number	Percent	Number	Percent
Lump-sum payment only	677	15.0	293	11.2	270	32.3	114	10.7
Weekly payments only	3,339	73.8	2,013	76.7	456	54.5	871	81.7
Both	202	4.5	140	5.3	23	2.8	39	3.7
None	307	6.8	179	6.8	87	10.4	42	3.9
Total	4,526	100.0	2,625	100.0	835	100.0	1,066	100.0
Missing cases	116							
Grand total	4,642							

Chi-square (unweighted) = 141.12** with 6 degrees of freedom.
Unlitigated cases are inflated by a factor of 3.583 to compensate for the smaller sampling ratio in the unlitigated sample.
Columns may not add to total due to rounding.

Table 2-17
Lump-Sum Payment (Gross) by Insurer Type

Lump-sum payment	Total		Insurer type					
			Carrier		Big three		Other self-insurers	
	Number	Percent	Number	Percent	Number	Percent	Number	Percent
$1 - $1,000	49	5.6	19	4.4	20	6.8	10	6.5
$1,001 - $2,000	109	12.4	50	11.5	34	11.6	25	16.3
$2,001 - $4,000	217	24.7	85	19.6	99	33.8	33	21.6
$4,001 - $8,000	206	23.4	90	20.8	89	30.4	27	17.6
$8,001 - $16,000	153	17.4	83	19.2	37	12.6	33	21.6
$16,001 - $32,000	125	14.2	88	20.3	14	4.8	23	15.0
Over $32,000	20	2.3	18	4.2	0	0	2	1.3
Total	879	100.0	433	100.0	293	100.0	153	100.0
			$\bar{X} = \$10,529$		$\bar{X} = \$5,659$		$\bar{X} = \$8,493$	
Missing cases	3,763							
Grand total	4,642							

Chi-square (unweighted) = 78.87** with 12 degrees of freedom.
Unlitigated cases are inflated by a factor of 3.583 to compensate for the smaller sampling ratio in the unlitigated sample.
Columns may not add to total due to rounding.

Table 2-18
Net Lump-Sum Payment by Insurer Type

| Lump-sum payment | Total | | Insurer type | | | | | |
| | | | Carrier | | Big three | | Other self-insurers | |
	Number	Percent	Number	Percent	Number	Percent	Number	Percent
$1 - $1,000	97	11.2	34	8.0	43	14.8	20	13.4
$1,001 - $2,000	146	16.8	68	15.9	50	17.2	28	18.8
$2,001 - $4,000	222	25.6	91	21.3	100	34.4	31	20.8
$4,001 - $8,000	195	22.5	97	22.7	68	23.4	30	20.1
$8,001 - $16,000	139	16.0	88	20.6	25	8.6	26	17.4
Over $16,000	68	7.8	49	11.5	5	1.7	14	9.4
Total	867	100.0	427	100.0	291	100.0	149	100.0
Missing cases	3,775		$\bar{X} = \$7,336$		$\bar{X} = \$3,777$		$\bar{X} = \$6,186$	
Grand total	4,642							

Chi-square (unweighted) = 59.54** with 10 degrees of freedom.
Unlitigated cases are inflated by a factor of 3.583 to compensate for the smaller sampling ratio in the unlitigated sample.
Columns may not add to total due to rounding.

There are even fewer really large lump-sums, although clearly they account for a significant proportion of the total lump-sum costs. Roughly 10 percent of lump-sum indemnity dollars go to the 2 percent of the lump-sum cases that receive over $32,000 in indemnity.

There are also considerable differences among the three insurer types in the size of lump-sum payments. This is borne out by the chi-square statistic, which shows that the null hypothesis of identical distributions can be rejected at a very high level of confidence. The distribution for the big three auto producers appears to be the most unique. It is very compact, with two-thirds of the cases falling between $2,000 and $8,000 in lump-sums. Presumably this reflects the ''routine retiree redemptions'' in the auto industry. It is said that there is an organized market for retiree redemptions in the auto industry. At any rate, the variance in size of lump-sum payments is considerably less for the big three than for other self-insurers or the carrier sector.

While table 2-16 showed that three times as many big three closed cases received lump-sum payments, table 2-17 indicates that the average lump-sum is much lower for the auto industry than for carriers or other self-insurers. This is noteworthy since the weekly compensation rate was shown to be significantly higher for the big three. It is hypothesized that this fact reflects the incidence of retiree redemptions in the auto industry also. These questions will be addressed more thoroughly later.

Table 2-19 presents the analysis of duration of disability payments when lump-sum payment cases are assigned imputed durations. After the deduction of legal costs and medical costs, each net lump-sum payment was divided by the average weekly indemnity payment to cases from the same insurer type to get a rough estimate of the number of weeks represented by the lump-sum payment. These imputed

Table 2-19
Estimated Duration of Disability by Insurer Type

| Duration of disability (actual or imputed) | Total | | Insurer type | | | | | |
| | | | Carrier | | Big three | | Other self-insurers | |
	Number	Percent	Number	Percent	Number	Percent	Number	Percent
Up to 26 weeks	3,474	82.9	2,014	83.3	564	75.5	896	87.5
26 to 52 weeks	298	7.1	149	6.2	98	13.1	51	5.0
1 year to 2 years	191	4.6	90	3.7	64	8.6	37	3.6
2 years to 4 years	136	3.2	98	4.0	11	1.5	27	2.6
Over 4 years	91	2.2	68	2.8	10	1.3	13	1.3
Total	4,190	100.0	2,419	100.0	748	100.0	1,024	100.0
			$\bar{X} = 23.6$		$\bar{X} = 23.7$		$\bar{X} = 16.9$	
Missing cases	452							
Grand total	4,642							

Chi-square (unweighted) = 51.90** with 8 degrees of freedom.
Unlitigated cases are inflated by a factor of 3.583 to compensate for the smaller sampling ratio in the unlitigated sample.
Columns may not add to total due to rounding.

durations were then added to any actual weekly payment durations for the individual claimant to yield a total estimated duration of disability.[9]

There are a number of interesting results shown in table 2-19. The dominance of short duration cases presented in table 2-14 is reduced. The inclusion of imputed durations for lump-sum cases has doubled the relative frequency of cases with more than 26 weeks disability duration, from 8 percent to 17 percent. There are also strong contrasts by insurer type apparent in table 2-19. The carrier segment experiences roughly twice as high a proportion of cases with more than two years estimated duration when compared to all self-insurers. The big three auto producers demonstrate the lowest relative incidence of long duration cases. They also show the lowest incidence of cases with less than 26 weeks estimated duration. This is accounted for by the fact that the bulk of the big three redemptions end up with imputed durations of between 26 weeks and two years.

The final point to be made about the estimated durations in table 2-19 is that the other self-insurers clearly demonstrate the lowest durations overall of any insurer type. The advantage they enjoyed in actual weekly payment durations (shown in table 2-14) has increased with the addition of the imputed durations from lump-sum cases. Table 2-19 shows that the average paid duration for self-insurers other than the big three is only 16.9 weeks, about 30 percent less than for other insurer types.

The last comparison to be presented is total indemnity for each closed case. Tables 2-20 and 2-21 show these results by insurer type. Table 2-20 reports the total indemnity *paid* to each closed case by insurer type. It adds the gross lump-sum amounts to total weekly compensation payments to arrive at the total indemnity paid to each closed case. Table 2-21, on the other hand, reports the total indemnity *received* by the

Table 2-20
Total Indemnity Paid by Insurer Type

| Total indemnity | Total | | Insurer type | | | | | |
| | | | Carrier | | Big three | | Other self-insurers | |
	Number	Percent	Number	Percent	Number	Percent	Number	Percent
None	307	6.8	179	6.8	87	10.4	42	3.9
$1 - $125	747	16.5	500	19.1	81	9.7	166	15.6
$126 - $250	196	4.3	147	5.6	12	1.4	37	3.5
$251 - $500	808	17.9	476	18.1	121	14.5	211	19.8
$501 - $1,000	728	16.1	426	16.2	104	12.5	198	18.6
$1,001 - $2,000	613	13.6	315	12.0	117	14.0	182	17.1
$2,001 - $4,000	463	10.2	215	8.2	142	17.1	106	9.9
$4,001 - $8,000	298	6.6	135	5.2	109	13.0	54	5.0
$8,001 - $16,000	169	3.7	91	3.5	42	5.0	37	3.4
$16,001 - $32,000	138	3.0	101	3.8	13	1.6	24	2.3
Over $32,000	58	1.3	40	1.5	8	1.0	10	0.9
Total	4,526	100.0	2,625	100.0	835	100.0	1,066	100.0
			$\bar{X} = \$2,862$		$\bar{X} = \$2,973$		$\bar{X} = \$2,275$	
Missing cases	117							
Grand total	4,642							

Chi-square (unweighted) = 124.79** with 20 degrees of freedom.
Unlitigated cases are inflated by a factor of 3.583 to compensate for the smaller sampling ratio in the unlitigated sample.
Columns may not add to total due to rounding.

Table 2-21
Total Indemnity Received by Insurer Type

| Total indemnity | Total | | Insurer type | | | | | |
| | | | Carrier | | Big three | | Other self-insurers | |
	Number	Percent	Number	Percent	Number	Percent	Number	Percent
None	316	7.0	182	6.9	89	10.6	46	4.3
$1 - $125	770	17.0	503	19.2	96	11.5	171	16.0
$126 - $250	202	4.5	149	5.7	13	1.5	40	3.7
$251 - $500	812	17.9	479	18.2	122	14.6	211	19.8
$501 - $1,000	743	16.4	433	16.5	110	13.2	200	18.8
$1,001 - $2,000	651	14.4	336	12.8	132	15.8	184	17.3
$2,001 - $4,000	465	10.3	218	8.3	142	17.1	105	9.8
$4,001 - $8,000	278	6.1	136	5.2	88	10.5	54	5.0
$8,001 - $16,000	155	3.4	95	3.6	30	3.5	31	2.9
$16,001 - $32,000	101	2.2	73	2.8	8	1.0	20	1.9
Over $32,000	32	0.7	21	0.8	6	0.7	5	0.5
Total	4,526	100.0	2,625	100.0	835	100.0	1,066	100.0
Missing cases	117		$\bar{X}$ = $2,319		$\bar{X}$ = $2,303		$\bar{X}$ = $1,921	
Grand total	4,642							

Chi-square (unweighted) = 92.08** with 20 degrees of freedom.
Unlitigated cases are inflated by a factor of 3.583 to compensate for the smaller sampling ratio in the unlitigated sample.
Columns may not add to total due to rounding.

claimants; it adds the net lump-sum payments and total weekly compensation payments. Both tables are presented for comparative purposes.

It is noteworthy that the big three and the carrier sector each come out with an average total indemnity payment of about $2,900, even though the distributions are quite different. The big three pay about twice as many claims in the $2,000 to $8,000 range as do other insurers. But they also show significantly more uncompensated cases. These facts presumably reflect the redemption policy of the auto industry. Other self-insurers have an average total indemnity level about 20 percent lower than either the carriers or the big three.

These figures represent the composite influence of the weekly compensation rates, the durations of weekly payments, the size of lump-sum payments, and the incidence of lump-sum payments. To simplify the comparisons, table 2-22 draws together all these elements in summary form. It is apparent that the three insurer types have widely differing workers' compensation experiences. The big three are clearly unique. They experience a very high litigation rate and a very high incidence of lump-sum payments, more than one-third of all closed cases according to the MCCS. They also have the highest proportion of uncompensated cases, presumably reflecting some successful defenses in the litigation process.

While they show by far the lowest proportion of weekly compensation (because of the influence of lump-sums), they pay the highest weekly compensation rates and the longest average durations. This results in an average weekly compensation figure that is about one-fourth higher than for the carrier segment. On the other hand, the big three appear to offset the remarkably high incidence of lump-sum payments with lower payments to each case. The net result is that the big three claimants receive the same average total indemnity per closed case as claimants in the carrier segment.

Table 2-22
Summary of Compensation by Insurer Type

Compensation summary	Carrier	Big three	Other self-insurers
Cases not compensated (Percent)	6.8	10.4	3.9
Cases with weekly compensation (Percent)	82.0	57.3	85.4
Average weekly compensation rate (Dollars per week)	127	144	139
Average weekly compensation duration (Weeks)	12.3	16.7	10.1
Average total weekly compensation (Dollars)	1,372	1,723	1,237
Cases with lump-sum payments (Percent)	16.5	35.1	14.4
Average gross lump-sum payments (Dollars)	10,529	5,659	8,493
Average net lump-sum payments (Dollars)	7,336	3,777	6,186
Average total indemnity paid (Dollars)	2,862	2,973	2,275
Average total indemnity received (Dollars)	2,319	2,303	1,921

Self-insurers other than the big three present a rather different picture. They have the highest proportion of weekly benefit payment cases and the lowest incidence of lump-sums. They also show the lowest proportion of uncompensated cases. The average weekly compensation rate for other self-insurers is 9 percent higher than for carriers, but they offset this with an 18 percent lower average duration; so the result is lower weekly indemnity costs. For lump-sum cases, they experience both a lower incidence and a lower average payment, yielding a substantial advantage in lump-sum payment costs. Summing all these elements, self-insurers other than the big three realize an average total indemnity figure that is 20 percent lower than both the carrier and the big three auto producer level.

NOTES

1. Inflating the samples to represent one year's cohort of closed cases was judged to be potentially misleading to the reader.

2. It might also be pointed out that the more inclusive the list of injuries, the greater the value of the redemption to the insurer since it prevents future claims for these same disabilities under terms of the redemption agreement.

3. The problem derives predominantly from the wage-loss philosophy of the Michigan statute. Since benefits are normally to be paid as long as wage loss continues, there is no need to create a categorization of disabilities as permanent or temporary. This will only become clear as time passes and wage loss continues or comes to an end.

4. *Michigan Statistical Abstract,* 14th Edition, 1979, pp. 286-87.

5. There is a fuller discussion of benefit payments in chapter 4.

6. For 1978, minimum benefits for full-time workers (more than 25 hours per week) ranged from $105 per week with no dependents to $120 with five or more dependents. Maximum benefits varied from $142 per week with no dependents to $171 with five or more. Similar ranges apply to the cases originating in the other injury years represented in table 2-12.

7. There is a full discussion of this issue in chapter 4.

8. Of course, the chi-square test is not a test of differences between means, but rather of the overall distribution as represented in the contingency table.

9. This procedure is the same one used in chapter 1 when comparing the MCCS to the NCCI Michigan Special Call sample.

LITIGATION

3

Introduction

As the term is used here, "litigation" refers to the filing of a formal, written request for a hearing with the Bureau of Workers' Disability Compensation.[1] It does not presume any outcome since many litigated cases do not even come to a hearing; 22 percent are withdrawn. So for the purposes of this discussion, "litigated" refers to the administrative treatment accorded the case, not to any particular resolution of the dispute. This chapter will examine the correlates of litigation in the Michigan workers' compensation system as revealed in the Michigan Closed Case Survey. The analysis will use the weighted sample so as to preserve the correct relationship between litigated and unlitigated cases in the population of workers' compensation cases.

In Michigan, litigated cases have come to form a "second system" of workers' compensation, which operates with entirely different procedures on very different types of claims. This examination of litigation in Michigan will prove to be frustrating because of the poor quality of information available. It will be necessary repeatedly to qualify factual statements, particularly involving litigated cases, due to the sources of the data. In most instances, all of the information available about a litigated case is the product of the litigation process. As such, it is intensely adversarial and of dubious validity.

Most litigated workers' compensation cases in Michigan enter the system with an attorney attached and no previous notice to the employer. It would be less common for a disability claim to "move over" to the litigated track because a dispute develops in the course of compensation. Most litigated cases end with a lump-sum redemption payment, i.e., a compromise and release agreement. It seems obvious in many cases that this was the objective all along. Thus the picture that emerges is of a weekly benefit system operating under the wage-loss principle for one set of claims, and a lump-sum compromise system operating informally as an impairment rating system for another set of claims. The lack of information about the basis for compensation in the latter cases prevents a clear judgment as to the adequacy or equity of the settlements. It also makes the description of those cases both difficult and unsatisfying. Nonetheless, it is important to make the attempt, even if the major result is to demonstrate how much is not known rather than how much is known.

First, a number of tables of bivariate results will be presented. These will examine the association of each of a number of case or claimant characteristics with the likelihood of litigation. This section will conclude with a multivariate analysis of the probability of litigation. The same basic variables used in the tabular analysis will all be considered simultaneously. The linear probability regression analysis will make possible the assessment of the impact of each variable on the likelihood of litigation, holding the other factors constant. This procedure, while suffering from some well-known technical flaws, reduces the errors associated with bivariate analysis when explanatory variables are intercorrelated.

In addition, a general description of the litigated case population will be presented. This is over and above the comparative picture of litigated cases that emerges from the discussion of the correlates of litigation. The first objective of the chapter is to make clear which cases are litigated. This analysis will then provide the setting for the description of the litigated case population as it is represented in the Michigan Closed Case Survey.

The Likelihood of Litigation

The first table is actually a repeat of table 2-1, except the focus is in the other direction. In chapter 2 the emphasis was on analysis of general case characteristics by insurer type; one of those characteristics was litigation status. Here the emphasis is on analysis of the likelihood of litigation, and one of the important correlates of litigation is insurer type (table 3-1). As discussed earlier, there are very significant differences in the likelihood of litigation among the different insurer types. The big three auto producers have a litigation rate that is more than double that of other self-insurers or the carrier sector.

It is important to point out that this does not necessarily prove the auto industry employers are more likely than others to contest a claim of given quality. It simply means that the frequency of claims that involve an application for hearing relative to those that do not is much higher for the auto industry. Since the overwhelming majority of applications for hearing are filed by claimants, this is more a description of the claims process in the auto industry than anything else. Nevertheless, it does produce a considerable administrative burden for the Bureau, inasmuch as all the litigation machinery is invoked with each new petition.

Table 3-2 presents the bivariate analysis of the association between the nature of the injury and the likelihood of litiga-

Table 3-1
Insurer Type by Litigation Status

| Insurer type | Total | | Litigation status | | | |
| | | | Unlitigated | | Litigated | |
	Number	Percent	Number	Percent	Number	Percent
Carrier	2,625	100.0	2,046	77.9	579	22.1
Big three	835	100.0	437	52.3	398	47.7
Other self-insurers	1,066	100.0	864	81.0	202	19.0
Total	4,526	100.0	3,347	73.9	1,179	26.1
Missing cases	117					
Grand total	4,642					

Chi-square (unweighted) = 118.21** with 2 degrees of freedom.

Unlitigated cases are inflated by a factor of 3.583 to compensate for the smaller sampling ratio in the unlitigated sample.

Rows may not add to total due to rounding.

Table 3-2
Nature of Injury by Litigation Status

Selected ANSI injury categories	Total		Litigation status			
			Unlitigated		Litigated	
	Number	Percent	Number	Percent	Number	Percent
Amputation	45	100.0	39	86.8	6	13.2
Burn	100	100.0	97	97.0	3	3.0
Bruise	566	100.0	462	81.6	104	18.4
Cut	427	100.0	412	96.5	15	3.5
Dislocation	62	100.0	54	87.0	8	13.0
Fracture	454	100.0	423	93.2	31	6.8
Hernia	165	100.0	147	89.1	18	10.9
Inflammation of joints	104	100.0	82	78.9	22	21.1
Sprain or strain	1,770	100.0	1,419	80.2	351	19.8
Multiple injuries	536	100.0	47	8.7	489	91.3
Other	310	100.0	150	48.5	160	51.5
Unclassified	70	100.0	64	91.5	6	8.5
Total	4,610	100.0	3,397	73.7	1,213	26.3
Missing cases	33					
Grand total	4,642					

Chi-square (unweighted) = 750.48** with 11 degrees of freedom.
Unlitigated cases are inflated by a factor of 3.583 to compensate for the smaller sampling ratio in the unlitigated sample.
Rows may not add to total due to rounding.

tion. Normally one would say the *effect* of the nature of injury on the likelihood of litigation, but the direction of causation is confused in this case. It has become the general practice to list as many injuries or impairments as possible in the belief that this increases the probability of an award, or perhaps the size of award. Thus, in a very real sense, the fact of litigation can affect the nature of injury claimed. This is particularly clear in the case of the coded category "multiple injuries" in table 3-2. If the multiple injuries are claimed because the case is being litigated rather than vice versa, the normal direction of causation is reversed. Thus it would not be proper to say that multiple injury claims are more likely to be resisted by insurers.

The same effect is evident in table 3-3, Injured Part of Body by Litigation Status. The parallel to multiple injuries is multiple parts of the body. The category "body system" is also strongly correlated with litigation. This fact reflects a reporting anomaly for occupational diseases in the Michigan system. Since the Petition for Hearing form filed by the claimant allows for the separate listing of a disablement due to occupational disease, this tends to be claimed as well. Again, this is a consequence of the adversary process, and not necessarily an unbiased assessment of the nature of the disabling condition. There is no unbiased review of the asserted facts before the hearing. For this reason, it is really not possible to accurately determine the incidence of occupational disease among Michigan's workers' compensation cases.

It is also impossible to determine the actual basis for the claim in most litigated cases in the MCCS. A review of the administrative record of the case, especially for redemptions where no transcript of the hearing is available, does not convey an adequate understanding of the basis for the decision. Thus the results in tables 3-2 and 3-3 must be treated very cautiously. While the chi-square statistics indicate great

Table 3-3
Injured Part of Body by Litigation Status

					Litigation status			
Part of body	Total		Unlitigated				Litigated	
	Number	Percent	Number	Percent			Number	Percent
Head or neck	153	100.0	125	81.7			28	18.3
Arm or wrist	311	100.0	287	92.3			24	7.7
Hand or finger	700	100.0	663	94.7			37	5.3
Abdomen	224	100.0	204	91.1			20	8.9
Back	1,037	100.0	795	76.7			242	23.3
Other trunk	254	100.0	236	92.9			18	7.1
Leg or ankle	589	100.0	548	93.0			41	7.0
Foot or toe	257	100.0	240	93.4			17	6.6
Multiple parts	872	100.0	236	27.1			636	72.9
Body system	173	100.0	36	20.7			137	79.3
Other	44	100.0	32	72.9			12	27.1
Total	4,616	100.0	3,404	73.7			1,212	26.3
Missing cases	26							
Grand total	4,642							

Chi-square (unweighted) = 798.81** with 10 degrees of freedom.

Unlitigated cases are inflated by a factor of 3.583 to compensate for the smaller sampling ratio in the unlitigated sample.

Rows may not add to total due to rounding.

statistical significance of the results, this is at least partially an artifact of the measurement of the actual characteristics of the case. All of the evidence available on some cases is generated by the adversarial litigation process itself, and this clearly affects the reporting of the "facts" in the case. Unfortunately, there is no way around this problem.

This measurement problem is also reflected in table 3-4 which reports the litigated proportions according to whether the claimant had been hospitalized in connection with the injury or illness. Over 90 percent of the cases where it could not be determined whether hospitalization had occurred were litigated cases. Among the cases where a determination could be made, table 3-4 indicates that when hospitalization occurred, the chance of litigation was higher. Regrettably, it cannot be reliably determined in which cases the insurer paid the cost of hospitalization, either through workers' compensation benefits or general health insurance programs. No case by case accounting for medical benefit payments is required by the Bureau of Workers' Disability Compensation. Thus it cannot be ascertained which hospitalizations are connected with directly compensable disabilities and which are connected with general conditions later determined, through the adversary process, to be compensable.

Table 3-5 indicates that the likelihood of litigation is inversely related to the reported weekly earnings. However, this is partly due to the closed case sampling design, combined with the long litigation delays in the Michigan system. The reported weekly earnings at the time of the injury will be lower for litigated cases simply because they are one to two years older at the time of closure, due solely to the litigation proceedings. Again in this instance, the fact that the null hypothesis of equality in earnings can be rejected is not a very meaningful result.

Table 3-4
Hospitalization by Litigation Status

Hospitalization status	Total		Litigation status			
			Unlitigated		Litigated	
	Number	Percent	Number	Percent	Number	Percent
Not hospitalized	3,285	100.0	2,745	83.6	540	16.4
Hospitalized	904	100.0	591	65.4	313	34.6
Unknown	396	100.0	32	8.1	364	91.9
Total	4,585	100.0	3,368	73.5	1,217	26.5
Missing cases	57					
Grand total	4,642					

Chi-square (unweighted) = 501.72** with 2 degrees of freedom.

Unlitigated cases are inflated by a factor of 3.583 to compensate for the smaller sampling ratio in the unlitigated sample.

Rows may not add to total due to rounding.

Table 3-5
Weekly Earnings by Litigation Status

Weekly earnings categories	Total		Litigation status			
			Unlitigated		Litigated	
	Number	Percent	Number	Percent	Number	Percent
To $100	211	100.0	154	73.0	57	27.0
$101 - $200	1,225	100.0	856	69.9	369	30.1
$201 - $300	1,582	100.0	1,154	72.9	428	27.1
$301 - $400	780	100.0	677	86.8	103	13.2
$401 - $500	284	100.0	254	89.5	30	10.5
Over $500	132	100.0	122	92.4	10	7.6
Total	4,215	100.0	3,218	76.3	997	23.7
Missing cases	428		$\bar{X} = \$263$		$\bar{X} = \$231$	
Grand total	4,642					

Chi-square (unweighted) = 62.34** with 5 degrees of freedom.

Unlitigated cases are inflated by a factor of 3.583 to compensate for the smaller sampling ratio in the unlitigated sample.

Rows may not add to total due to rounding.

There is more certainty about the numbers presented in table 3-6. They show the proportion litigated according to the geographic origin of the claim; the litigiousness of Detroit is readily apparent. In chapter 2 it was pointed out that Detroit cases made up 55 percent of all Michigan workers' compensation cases. But among litigated cases, Detroit accounts for over 70 percent. This results from a 36.6 percent litigation rate among Detroit area cases, compared to 22.2 percent for the balance of the state. The least litigious areas according to table 3-6 are Muskegon, Kalamazoo-Portage, Grand Rapids, and Lansing. All experience litigation rates under 15 percent. The chi-square statistic shows that the sample evidence is strong enough to reject the hypothesis of no difference in likelihood of litigation among locations.

Turning to claimant characteristics, table 3-7 reveals that females appear to have a marginally higher litigation proportion. But the chi-square statistic is not significant; meaning that the hypothesis of equality cannot be rejected. Table 3-8 demonstrates that age of the claimant, however, is significantly correlated with the likelihood of litigation. The age distributions of claimants in litigated and unlitigated cases are markedly different, with the probability of litigation rising after age 50. This represents the effect of the "retiree problem" in Michigan workers' compensation. It may also reflect the incidence of occupational disease which tends to rise with age.

While the Michigan system is ostensibly a wage-loss system, claims from retirees have long been a serious problem. Virtually all retiree claims are redeemed, i.e., settled by compromise and release. Some allege that most of them are paid because of their "nuisance value"; it is cheaper to pay a few thousand dollars to redeem the case than to incur the cost of effectively defending against the claim. The redemption has the added value from the insurer's point of view of

Table 3-6
Geographical Location of Injury by Litigation Status

SMSA of injury	Total		Litigation status			
			Unlitigated		Litigated	
	Number	Percent	Number	Percent	Number	Percent
Ann Arbor-Ypsilanti	146	100.0	111	76.0	35	24.0
Battle Creek	61	100.0	50	82.0	11	18.0
Detroit	2,355	100.0	1,494	63.4	861	36.6
Flint	247	100.0	183	74.1	64	25.9
Grand Rapids	340	100.0	290	85.3	50	14.7
Jackson	64	100.0	50	78.2	14	21.8
Kalamazoo-Portage	113	100.0	97	85.8	16	14.2
Lansing-East Lansing	156	100.0	133	85.2	23	14.8
Muskegon	99	100.0	86	86.9	13	13.1
Saginaw	109	100.0	82	75.3	27	24.7
Other	580	100.0	484	83.4	96	16.6
Total	4,270	100.0	3,060	71.7	1,210	28.3
Missing cases	372					
Grand total	4,642					

Chi-square (unweighted) = 90.55** with 10 degrees of freedom.
Unlitigated cases are inflated by a factor of 3.583 to compensate for the smaller sampling ratio in the unlitigated sample.
Rows may not add to total due to rounding.

Table 3-7
Gender by Litigation Status

| | Total | | Litigation status | | | |
| | | | Unlitigated | | Litigated | |
Gender	Number	Percent	Number	Percent	Number	Percent
Male	3,556	100.0	2,637	74.2	919	25.8
Female	1,075	100.0	778	72.4	297	27.6
Total	4,631	100.0	3,415	73.7	1,216	26.3
Missing cases	12					
Grand total	4,642					

Chi-square (unweighted) = 0.60 with 1 degrees of freedom.

Unlitigated cases are inflated by a factor of 3.583 to compensate for the smaller sampling ratio in the unlitigated sample.

Rows may not add to total due to rounding.

Table 3-8
Age at Injury by Litigation Status

| | Total | | Litigation status | | | |
| | | | Unlitigated | | Litigated | |
Age	Number	Percent	Number	Percent	Number	Percent
Through 20	411	100.0	362	88.1	49	11.9
21 to 30	1,206	100.0	967	80.2	239	19.8
31 to 40	861	100.0	699	81.2	162	18.8
41 to 50	672	100.0	505	75.2	167	24.8
51 to 60	664	100.0	398	59.9	266	40.1
Over 60	280	100.0	72	25.6	208	74.4
Total	4,094	100.0	3,003	73.3	1,091	26.7
Missing cases	549					
Grand total	4,642					

Chi-square (unweighted) = 229.73** with 5 degrees of freedom.

Unlitigated cases are inflated by a factor of 3.583 to compensate for the smaller sampling ratio in the unlitigated sample.

Rows may not add to total due to rounding.

forestalling any additional claim from the individual involved, providing the language describing the injury is sufficient-
ly broad to encompass any possible compensable injury.

For the litigated closed case sample, an attempt was made
to determine the retirement status of the claimant from the
information contained in the official case file. The coders,
all experienced former Bureau of Workers' Disability Compensation employees, found they were able to make a
reasonably certain determination in about three-fourths of
all litigated cases. The remainder were recorded as unknown.
Table 3-9 shows that at least one-fourth of the litigated cases
definitely did involve a retired claimant. If one assumes that
the unknown category can be divided between retired and
nonretired workers according to the proportions in the rest
of the sample, the proportion of retirees rises to 35 percent.

The table also reveals very significant differences by insurer type. A minimum of 42 percent of litigated big three
cases are from retirees (it would be 53 percent under the same
allocative assumption about the unknowns). On the other
hand, only 14 percent of litigated carrier claimants are
retired (rising to 20 percent with allocation of unknowns).
This means that the auto industry has up to three times the
relative incidence of retiree claims. The other self-insurer
group falls in between with an estimated range of 29 to 40
percent retiree claims. So the evidence in the MCCS suggests
that 40 to 50 percent of litigated claims in the auto industry,
30 to 40 percent of litigated claims from other self-insurers,
and 15 to 20 percent of litigated carrier claims are from
retired employees.

Table 3-10 suggests that the results are similar for total indemnity costs. Approximately $9 million in indemnity was
paid to the 1,224 litigated cases in the sample over the active
span of those cases, i.e., before closure. At least one-fourth
of this was paid to retirees; perhaps as much as one-third.

Table 3-9

Retirement Status by Insurer Type - Litigated Cases Only

Retirement status	Total		Insurer type					
			Carrier		Big three		Other self-insurers	
	Number	Percent	Number	Percent	Number	Percent	Number	Percent
Non-retired	522	48.2	307	57.3	136	37.0	79	43.9
Retired	285	26.3	77	14.4	155	42.1	53	29.4
Unknown	277	25.6	152	28.4	77	20.9	48	26.7
Total	1,084	100.0	536	100.0	368	100.0	180	100.0
Missing cases	140							
Grand total	1,224							

Chi-square (unweighted) = 89.09** with 4 degrees of freedom.

Columns may not add to total due to rounding.

Table 3-10

Total Indemnity Paid to Retirees by Insurer Type - Litigated Cases Only

Retired claimant?	Total		Insurer type					
			Carrier		Big three		Other self-insurers	
	Dollars	Percent	Dollars	Percent	Dollars	Percent	Dollars	Percent
No	4,197,457	47.8	3,016,105	56.2	615,751	32.0	565,601	38.1
Yes	2,279,967	26.0	798,055	14.9	990,745	51.5	491,167	33.1
Unknown	2,302,093	26.2	1,557,099	29.0	316,009	16.4	428,985	28.9
Total	8,779,517	100.0	5,371,259	100.0	1,922,505	100.0	1,485,753	100.0

Columns may not add to total due to rounding.

For carriers, the range is again about 15 to 20 percent; for the big three, 50 to 60 percent; and for other self-insurers, from 33 to 45 percent.

Of course, these indemnity amounts would be less when expressed as a proportion of *all* indemnity, not just that paid to litigated cases. Using the minimum proportions from table 3-9, payments to retirees represent *at least* 18 percent of all indemnity payments reported in the MCCS. This proportion ranges from a low of 10 percent for carriers to a high of 40 percent for the big three. Other self-insurers as a group pay roughly 20 percent of their indemnity dollars to retired claimants.

Table 3-11 shows that these litigated retiree claims are almost all redeemed. Less than 4 percent are resolved in some other manner. This contrasts with about 65 percent redeemed among those litigated cases where the claimant could not definitely be identified as a retiree. Retirees are receiving at least 28 percent of all lump-sum payments to Michigan workers' compensation claimants.

These numbers are very striking; but they do tend to overstate the magnitude of the retiree problem somewhat because of the bias of the closed case design. Lump-sum payments will be fully valued in the present as they are committed. The nature of the closed case design means that the long term weekly benefit cases will be both underestimated in number and undervalued in cost. Thus the current lump-sum payments to retirees are overvalued relative to the total indemnity base. The size of this bias is unclear, but it is worth noting that it should be offset to some degree by the opposite bias produced by the difficulty of actually identifying retirees in workers' compensation cases. Nevertheless, the evidence from the closed case sample is sufficient to demonstrate that payments to retirees are a very important factor in Michigan workers' compensation.

Table 3-11
Retirement Status by Method of Resolution
Litigated Cases Only

	Total		Resolution									
			Redeemed		Withdrawn		Dismissed		Accepted		Decision	
Retirement status	Number	Percent	Number	Percent	Number	Percent	Number	Percent	Number	Percent	Number	Percent
Non-retired	537	100.0	362	67.4	71	13.2	21	3.9	42	7.8	41	7.6
Retired	292	100.0	282	96.6	1	0.3	2	0.7	0	0.0	7	2.4
Unknown	290	100.0	174	60.0	54	18.6	32	11.0	10	3.4	20	6.9
Total	1,119	100.0	818	73.1	126	11.3	55	4.9	52	4.6	68	6.1
Missing cases	105											
Grand total	1,224											

Chi-square = 146.8** with 8 degrees of freedom.

Rows may not add to total due to rounding.

Redemption payments to retirees are of interest because of their clear conflict with the wage-loss philosophy of compensation. The major principle of wage loss is that income maintenance payments shall be made as long as wage loss continues. This can be contrasted with an impairment philosophy where injured workers are compensated for the injury itself as well as, or instead of, the loss of wages attendant upon the injury. In the case of a voluntarily retired claimant, it would seem fairly obvious that no wage loss is being suffered even though there may be an impairment of some kind. This is one reason for the assertion that the litigation system in Michigan can be regarded as a second workers' compensation system.

Multivariate Analysis

Table 3-12 presents the multivariate analysis of the correlates of litigation. It reports the result of a simple linear probability regression with a dichotomous dependent variable, whether the case was litigated or it was not. The independent or explanatory variables are the same ones discussed in the tabular results above, with a few exceptions. The goal is to estimate the impact of each characteristic on the likelihood of litigation, holding all other factors included in the model constant.

In those instances where the independent variable is categorical, the linear probability regression measures the marginal impact of the presence of the characteristic as compared to the alternative state of the world, namely the absence of the characteristic. Where the categories would exhaust all the alternatives, one category has been omitted and serves as the reference group. For insurer type, carriers are the omitted group and the marginal impact of the big three or other self-insurer is measured against that of carriers.

Table 3-12
Probability of Litigation
Linear Probability Regression

	Dependent variable - probability of litigation p(LIT) = .264			
$\overline{X}$	Independent variables	$\hat{\beta}$	se	t
.507	Detroit	.101	.015	6.92**
.180	Big three	.075	.028	2.69**
.230	Other self-insurers	-.058	.016	3.63**
.114	Detroit and big three	.008	.035	.24
.146	Age (55 or over)	.103	.022	4.77**
.040	Age and big three	.053	.043	1.22
.232	Female	.014	.015	.90
2.212	Indemnity ($1,000's)	.024	.001	18.54**
.054	Multiple spells	.036	.030	1.21
.011	Fatality	.169	.065	2.61**
.022	Burn	-.094	.045	2.09*
.092	Cut	-.061	.024	2.55*
.098	Fracture	-.064	.023	2.78**
.022	Inflammation	.047	.044	1.07
.115	Multiple injuries	.336	.029	11.50**
.067	Other injuries	.079	.034	2.32*
.224	Back injuries	.112	.018	6.36**
.188	Multiple parts	.303	.024	12.82**
.037	Body system	.466	.045	10.39**
	Constant	.002		

n = 2,177

$F_{(19, 2157)} = 134.87$**

$R^2 = .543$

Ordinary least squares estimation with a dichotomous dependent variable is known to produce heteroscedastic error terms. The estimates are unbiased, but not efficient.[2] That is, the estimated coefficients are accurate, but the standard errors of those coefficients are biased upward. This means that the standard t-test of statistical significance of the coefficients is made more difficult; it is possible that statistically significant results will be incorrectly judged to be insignificant.

In the present application, this flaw was not judged to be serious enough to mandate the use of nonlinear techniques. The interest here is in a broad assessment of the association of various case and claimant characteristics with the fact of litigation. Linear probability is sufficient for that purpose, even though it is not the optimal estimation procedure in this situation. It is possible that some weak relationships will be judged to be insignificant as a result, but in the face of the measurement problems and causation problems discussed earlier, this is not too serious.

The regression was performed on a weighted sample of MCCS cases, but in this instance the weights are not the same as employed earlier. Here it is critical that the total number of actual observations not be overstated. This would make the overall regression appear more significant than is warranted. So the weights are chosen to make the total number of observations coincide with the actual, while at the same time preserving the relation between litigated and unlitigated cases. This necessitated weighting each unlitigated case by a factor of 1.680 and each litigated case by .469. The result is a weighted sample of 574 litigated and 1,603 unlitigated cases. The litigated case population is thereby kept to 26 percent of the total, and the total number of weighted cases is held to 2,177 (actual was 2,178).

The left-hand column in table 3-12 reports the sample mean for each variable. In the case of dichotomous variables such as Detroit, where the variable takes on the value 1 if the claim is from Detroit and 0 otherwise, this mean is the proportion of cases in the sample that have the characteristic. For Detroit the mean is .507, which indicates that just over 50 percent of the cases originate in Detroit. The regression coefficient ($\hat{\beta}$) then reports the marginal impact of the presence of this characteristic on the probability that the case will be litigated.

One of the advantages of linear probability estimates is that the coefficients are readily interpreted in straight probability terms. Thus in table 3-12 the estimated coefficient for Detroit, listed first in the table, indicates that the probability of litigation for a claim which originates in Detroit is .101 higher than one originating elsewhere in the state, holding other factors constant. In other words, Detroit cases are 10 percent more likely to be litigated than cases from the balance of the state. Furthermore, the t-test indicates that it is possible to reject the null hypothesis that a Detroit origin is not correlated with the likelihood of litigation at a 99 percent level of confidence.

It is important to emphasize that the coefficient measures the *marginal* impact, i.e., holding all other factors included in the estimated equation constant. It was reported earlier in this chapter that 36.6 percent of Detroit cases were litigated while only 22.2 percent of other cases were; implying that Detroit cases are 14.4 percent more likely to be litigated. This is a gross difference, however, and it does not hold any other factors constant. The measurement reported in table 3-12 is an estimate of the marginal or net impact of Detroit origin on litigation likelihood. It is lower than the gross because Detroit claimants are more likely to have other characteristics associated with litigation, e.g., work in the auto industry.

Similar observations can be made about the impact of the next variable in table 3-12, the big three. The estimated equation indicates that cases from the big three have a probability of litigation that is .075 higher than those where a carrier handles the coverage (the omitted category). On the other hand, the coefficient for other self-insurers indicates that they are less likely (by .058) to experience litigation than are the carriers. In both instances these are marginal results, holding the other factors in the regression equation constant, and in both cases the null hypothesis of no relationship can be rejected by conventional statistical standards. The result for the big three means that the earlier results reported in table 3-1 seriously overstated the impact of the big three on the likelihood of litigation. Only about one-third of the gross difference shown in table 3-1 was actually due to the insurer type. The other two-thirds was due to other factors, such as the greater incidence of retiree claims.

The next variable is designed to measure interaction between location and insurer. It tests for the possibility that there is a synergistic, or interactive, litigation effect on a claim from the big three that originates in the Detroit area. The hypothesis is that the presence of both these factors leads to a higher tendency to litigate than the simple sum of the previous coefficients. This variable takes the value 1 if the claim is from the Detroit area *and* is against one of the big three auto producers and 0 otherwise. The mean value at the left indicates that 11.4 percent of all closed cases do share these two characteristics. But the coefficient for this variable is not significantly different from zero, which indicates that the hypothesis of interaction can be rejected.

The variable labeled "Age 55 or over" serves as a proxy for the retiree issue. Since retirement status was not gathered for the unlitigated cases, it was necessary to approximate this variable. Age 55 was chosen as the lower terminus of the "early" retirement age group. Clearly, this amounts to a dilution of the influence of retired status since there are many active workers between ages 55 and 65. However, due to the "30 years and out" possibility in the auto industry, there are a fairly significant number of retirements that occur in the mid to late 50s.

The coefficient for age 55 or over indicates that this age group has a rate of litigation that is about 10 percent higher than for younger workers. Even measured as imperfectly as it is, this factor appears to be as important as a Detroit origin in producing litigation. It is relatively more influential than being employed in the auto industry, at least as estimated in this equation. In addition, there is another interaction term in the equation which tests whether there is a synergistic effect between the big three and older workers. In other words, is the probability of litigation even higher when the claimant is an older auto worker? The results in table 3-12 do not confirm this. While the coefficient appears to be positive, the t-test shows that it is not significantly different from zero. Thus the interaction hypothesis has to be rejected. These results reinforce those presented earlier in this chapter. Older workers are much more likely to be involved in litigated claims. One can only speculate that if retirement status were more adequately measured, the relationship would be even stronger than revealed here.

The last variable in the group of background variables is the gender of the claimant. The female variable measures the differential probability of litigation as a correlate of the sex of the claimant. Table 3-12 reveals that there is no significant difference between men (the omitted category) and women in terms of litigation of workers' compensation claims.

The second group of independent variables refers directly to the workers' compensation case itself rather than to the claimant or the insurer. In a sense, these variables attempt to measure the elements of the claim that are associated with an elevated tendency to litigate. The first of these is the level of indemnity payments for the claim. Since the sample is composed of closed cases, the indemnity cost is known with certainty, subject only to the possibility of reopening at some future date. The level of indemnity is measured in units of one thousand dollars, so the estimated coefficient indicates that for each thousand dollars of indemnity paid, the probability of litigation increases by .024. The t-statistic indicates that it is possible to reject the hypothesis of no relationship between the likelihood of litigation and the level of indemnity paid.

What the t-statistic cannot do is indicate the *direction* of causation. One can say that there is a relationship, it is not possible to say in which direction the causation flows.[3] In particular, it may well be that the process of litigation itself contributes to the level of indemnity. On the other hand, the litigation may be a normal outgrowth of the complications attending the more serious disability claims. Then one would find a relationship between the level of indemnity and litigation, even though they both are consequences of the seriousness of the disability. In the next chapter, multivariate results on the determinants of indemnity will be presented, but this issue of causation will still not be firmly laid to rest because of the general lack of unbiased information about litigated cases. One conclusion, however, is firm; there is a positive relationship between the amount of indemnity paid and the probability of litigation in Michigan's workers' compensation system.

The variable for "multiple spells" represents an attempt to try to control for the difficult cases. This dichotomous variable takes the value 1 if there was more than one distinct period of disability associated with the claim. It should be noted that this includes the possibilities of a reinjury or an aggravation of a pre-existing injury, as well as a relapse or premature return to work. This variable is also subject to measurement problems in that it is possible that dubious litigated claims show a tendency to cite earlier periods of disability to increase the credibility of the claim. This could be analogous to the measurement problems with the nature of injury discussed earlier. A somewhat surprising proportion of all closed cases do report more than one period of disability—over 5 percent according to table 3-12. However, this factor is not significantly related to the probability of litigation; the hypothesis of no relationship cannot be rejected in this case.

The rest of the independent variables relate to the asserted cause of the claim, the specific injury or illness that produced the disability. For litigated cases, this information comes from the claimant, generally with the assistance of an attorney. For unlitigated cases, the information comes from the employer. It is very clear that the nature of the injury and part of body reported in litigated cases are designed to influence the outcome of th litigation process. Thus the measurement problems complicate the interpretation of these results; it is once again prudent to emphasize association rather than causation in this discussion.

According to the estimated linear probability regression equation reported in table 3-12, fatality claims are significantly more likely to be litigated than are non-fatality cases. While the mean indicates that only about 1 percent of all claims are for fatalities, the estimated coefficient shows that they are much more likely to be litigated. In fact, this coefficient is the largest discussed so far; a fatality claim increases the likelihood of litigation by .169. Presumably these disputes are over the question of work-relatedness of the fatality. It will be shown later that most of these cases are settled with lump-sum payments.

The next six variables refer to the nature of injury categories reported earlier in table 3-2. The three categories with the highest litigation tendency (multiple injuries, other injuries, and inflammation of joints) and the three with the lowest (burns, cuts, and fractures) from that table are entered as dichotomous variables. In each instance the estimated coefficient measures the marginal contribution of that injury type to the probability of litigation. The comparison group consists of the omitted categories (amputation, bruise, dislocation, hernia, sprain or strain, and unclassified). It can be seen in table 3-12 that the burn, cut, and fracture categories all are associated with reduced probability of litigation. Inflammation of joints is not significant, the hypothesis of no relationship cannot be rejected. Other injuries are positively correlated with litigation. All these coefficients are in the 5 to 10 percent range, a meaningful level of association but smaller than those discussed heretofore.

The coefficient for multiple injuries, on the other hand, is very large. Table 3-12 indicates that a claim of multiple injuries is associated with an increase of .336 in the probability of litigation. This reflects the now familiar problem of the dependence of the observations of litigated cases on the litigation process itself. There is a high correlation between claiming multiple injuries and litigation because that is the way it is done in Michigan. Thus it may be not so much that multiple injuries lead to a contested claim as it is that a litigated claim asserts multiple injuries to increase the chance of a settlement.

The same is true of the remaining variables in the regression that refer to the part of the body involved in the injury or disease. Multiple body parts and body system involvement are almost synonymous with litigated claims in Michigan; the direction of causation is unclear here as well. "Back injuries" are also reported in table 3-12 to be correlated with an elevated probability of litigation. Back injuries were the single largest group in table 3-3 presented earlier. Here it is shown that an injury to the back is associated with an increase of .112 in the probability of litigation. This result is apart from the tendency for back injuries to also be included among the multiple injury and multiple parts of the body. It is perhaps to be expected that there would be a greater tendency for litigation in back injuries because of the difficulty of establishing the fact of disability objectively.

In summary, it has been demonstrated here that a claim of multiple injuries is very strongly correlated with litigation in workers' compensation cases. But this may be more a *consequence* of litigation than a *precipitator* of litigation. There is a certain stylized way of pursuing a redemption settlement in Michigan, and the claim of multiple injuries is a part of it. The same holds true for an injury involving an entire body system, since this covers the circulatory system (heart cases), the respiratory system (lung cases) and other occupational disease claims. Again, it has become conventional to claim these kinds of involvements in litigated claims.

In a more productive sense, it has been determined that fatalities are more prone to litigation than other cases; that Detroit claims are more likely to be litigated, as are those originating from claimants 55 or more years of age, and those from employees of the big three auto producers. Higher indemnity levels are associated with greater litigation probability and so are back injuries. On the other hand, straightforward injuries like burns, cuts, and fractures are less likely to lead to litigation. It was also shown that self-insurers other than the big three are significantly less likely to be involved in litigated cases.

Having described to the limits of the data base which cases are likely to be litigated, attention will turn now to a description of the litigated cases as a group.

The Litigation Process

This section will address the origin of litigated cases and some of their administrative characteristics. Questions such as who initiated the litigation, how many insurers and employers were involved, what sorts of injuries were claimed, and what was the outcome of the litigation will be covered. The major benefit delivery issues, namely the amount of indemnity paid, in what form, and when it was paid will be deferred until the next chapter. For the remainder of this chapter, the discussion will relate only to litigated cases. As before, the major discriminating variable will be the type of insurer.

Table 3-13 shows that almost all litigated cases "originate" with a petition from the employee. This does not mean that the employer has no role in precipitating disputes; the employer may reject the claim and then wait for the employee to take the initiative in pressing his or her claim further. The other category of table 3-13 that contains a significant number of cases, agreement to redeem, represents a slightly different approach. In these cases the parties have already come to an agreement on a compromise and release settlement. However, since the Bureau of Workers' Disability Compensation must approve all redemptions, this agreement requires a hearing and approval before it can take effect.

The question of the employer's knowledge and anticipation of litigated claims is a difficult one, especially with retired claimants. It is asserted by employers in Michigan that many litigated claims appear "out of the blue," and that in some cases it is a major challenge just to discover whether the claimant was ever an employee or not. Table 3-14 lends some credence to these assertions. In Michigan, Form 100, Employer's Basic Report of Injury, is required for all injuries, including diseases, which arise out of and in the course of the employment and cause (1) an aggregate of seven or more days of disability; (2) death; or (3) specific losses as enumerated in the statute. This requirement is designed to insure that the Bureau is informed of every com-

Table 3-13
Reason for Hearing by Insurer Type

Reason for hearing	Total		Insurer type					
			Carrier		Big three		Other self-insurers	
	Number	Percent	Number	Percent	Number	Percent	Number	Percent
Petition by employee	1,137	96.7	550	95.2	396	99.7	191	95.0
Petition by employer	3	0.3	2	0.3	0	0.0	1	0.5
Agreement to redeem	25	2.1	18	3.1	0	0.0	7	3.5
Application for advance	2	0.2	1	0.2	0	0.0	1	0.5
Other	9	0.8	7	1.2	1	0.3	1	0.5
Total	1,176	100.0	578	100.0	397	100.0	201	100.0
Missing cases	48							
Grand total	1,224							

Chi-square (unweighted) = 20.08** with 8 degrees of freedom.

Columns may not add to total due to rounding.

pensable accident or illness. In the event that no subsequent report of compensation is received, the Bureau inquires as to the reason.

Table 3-14 shows that in the majority of litigated cases, Form 100 was never filed. Approximately 64 percent of carrier, 74 percent of other self-insurer, and 80 percent of big three litigated cases do not contain the Employer's Basic Report of Injury in the official case file. These numbers probably overstate the fact to some degree, since it is reasonable to suppose that mistakes in filing are made. This is especially true given the sketchy information about earlier injuries sometimes offered in an employee's Petition for Hearing. However, it does seem clear that the majority of litigated claims have not been previously reported to the Bureau.

There is no other way of determining what the employer's knowledge of the situation may have been before being served with the Petition for Hearing. But the employer does have one powerful motive to report any incidents. In Michigan, the statute of limitations for workers' compensation cases does not begin to toll until the accident is reported to the Bureau. If an employer knows of an incident which might lead to a claim, it is in his or her interest to report it. Thus it seems reasonable to conclude that many of these claims do come as a surprise to the employer when no Form 100 has been filed.

This conclusion is further buttressed by table 3-15 which shows that in over 80 percent of litigated cases, the dispute comes first. That is, there are no weekly compensation benefits paid before the initiation of the litigation process. The litigated cases are not those where a dispute develops over the long-run consequences of a clearly disabling injury; they seem rather to be cases where the dispute is over whether there is any disablement at all, or over the cause of that disablement. In a sense, the dispute is over whether

Table 3-14
Form 100 Status by Insurer Type

| Form 100 status | Total | | Insurer type | | | | | |
| | | | Carrier | | Big three | | Other self-insurers | |
	Number	Percent	Number	Percent	Number	Percent	Number	Percent
Form 100 not filed	825	71.1	363	63.6	314	80.7	148	74.0
Form 100-first injury	304	26.2	193	33.8	65	16.7	46	23.0
Form 100-subsequent injury	11	0.9	10	1.8	1	0.3	0	0.0
Form 100-multiple injuries	20	1.7	5	0.9	9	2.3	6	3.0
Total	1,160	100.0	571	100.0	389	100.0	200	100.0
Missing cases	64							
Grand total	1,224							

Chi-square (unweighted) = 49.48** with 8 degrees of freedom.
Columns may not add to total due to rounding.

Table 3-15
Timing of Dispute by Insurer Type

Timing of dispute	Total		Insurer type					
			Carrier		Big three		Other self-insurers	
	Number	Percent	Number	Percent	Number	Percent	Number	Percent
Dispute before compensation	930	82.2	411	75.0	367	93.4	152	79.6
Compensation before dispute	202	17.8	137	25.0	26	6.6	39	20.4
Total	1,132	100.0	548	100.0	393	100.0	191	100.0
Missing cases	92							
Grand total	1,224							

Chi-square (unweighted) = 53.80** with 2 degrees of freedom.
Columns may not add to total due to rounding.

there is a legitimate claim. Table 3-15 shows that this is even more true of the auto industry.

On the other hand, these claims sometimes are inherently complicated. Table 3-16 reports that about 10 percent of litigated claims involve multiple insurers, multiple employers, or both. These cases are naturally going to be more difficult because of the extra factual questions introduced by the multiple liability possibility. In addition, table 3-17 shows that about one-fourth of the litigated cases involve more than one injury date. This too would contribute to the potential for dispute as the facts are clouded by multiple causation or reinjury issues. The chi-square statistic indicates that these experiences are similar for all three insurer types.

Table 3-16
Number of Different Insurers
and Employers Involved

	Number of employers	
Number of insurers	**One**	**More than one**
One insurer	1,105	2
	(90.3%)	(0.2%)
Multiple self-insurers	0	14
	-	(1.1%)
Multiple carriers	52	51
	(4.2%)	(4.2%)
Total	1,157	67
	(94.5%)	(5.5%)

Table 3-18, however, demonstrates that when the number of injuries is added to the table, the results are changed materially. Apparently the self-insurers experience a larger number of claimed injuries even though these do not occur on separate dates. A narrow majority of litigated cases for

Table 3-17
Separate Injury Days Reported by Insurer Type

Separate injury days reported	Total		Insurer type					
			Carrier		Big three		Other self-insurers	
	Number	Percent	Number	Percent	Number	Percent	Number	Percent
One	854	73.9	421	73.5	294	76.0	139	70.9
Two	253	21.9	124	21.6	79	20.4	50	25.5
Three	49	4.2	28	4.9	14	3.6	7	3.6
Total	1,156	100.0	573	100.0	387	100.0	196	100.0
Missing cases	68							
Grand total	1,224							

Chi-square (unweighted) = 3.18 with 4 degrees of freedom.
Columns may not add to total due to rounding.

Table 3-18
Number of Injuries and Injury Dates by Insurer Type

Number of injuries and injury dates	Total		Insurer type					
			Carrier		Big three		Other self-insurers	
	Number	Percent	Number	Percent	Number	Percent	Number	Percent
One injury, one date	516	53.3	333	58.1	189	48.8	94	48.0
Two injuries, one date	212	18.3	80	14.0	90	23.3	42	21.4
Two injuries, two dates	228	19.7	113	19.7	69	17.8	46	23.5
Three injuries, one date	26	2.2	8	1.4	15	3.9	3	1.5
Three injuries, three dates	49	4.2	28	4.9	14	3.6	7	3.6
Three injuries, two dates	25	2.2	11	1.9	10	2.6	4	2.0
Total	1,156	100.0	573	100.0	387	100.0	196	100.0
Missing cases	68							
Grand total	1,224							

Chi-square (unweighted) = 31.67** with 12 degrees of freedom.

Columns may not add to total due to rounding.

both the big three and other self-insurers involve either multiple injuries or multiple injury dates. Of course these results reflect the data gathering process, and they do substantially understate the actual number of injuries mentioned by the claimant on the Petition for Hearing. The figures reported here represent the best judgment of the coders as to what actual injury lay behind the claim. Therefore, they stand somewhere between established fact and simple transmittal of claimant assertions. As was discussed earlier, there is no way to review litigated cases in Michigan more adequately using official records. The exact nature of the injury, being the primary basis of contention, remains obscured by the litigation process.

Table 3-19 reports, for the same injuries tabulated in tables 3-17 and 3-18, the type of injury claimed, whether personal injury or occupational disease. This categorization is provided by the claimant and may be subject to some question, since no review is conducted. The Petition for Hearing form provides separate lines for entering the date of occurrence of personal injury or occupational disease, and it is likely that this tends to elicit more occupational disease claims than would be forthcoming under other circumstances. Inasmuch as the line is on the form, some claimants probably are motivated to fill it in with the hope of increasing the likelihood of an award or compromise settlement.

Analysis of the type of injury claimed, however, does show that about one-fourth of all litigated cases involve *purely* occupational disease claims. A total of nearly 60 percent claim to suffer *some* occupational disease, while just over 40 percent claim personal injuries only. Furthermore, there are rather striking differences by insurer type. The proportion of occupational disease claims is much higher among the self-insured population. Over 70 percent of the big three cases and over 60 percent of other self-insurer cases involve

Table 3-19
Type of Injury by Insurer Type

Type of injury	Total		Insurer type					
			Carrier		Big three		Other self-insurers	
	Number	Percent	Number	Percent	Number	Percent	Number	Percent
Personal injury only	483	41.7	295	51.8	112	28.8	76	38.4
Occupational disease only	296	25.6	107	18.8	144	37.0	45	22.7
Both	378	32.7	168	29.5	133	34.2	77	38.9
Total	1,157	100.0	570	100.0	389	100.0	198	100.0
Missing cases	67							
Grand total	1,224							

Chi-square (unweighted) = 65.10** with 4 degrees of freedom.
Columns may not add to total due to rounding.

some claim of occupational disease, compared to about 50 percent of carrier cases.

While it is possible that self-insurers do experience higher rates of occupational diseases, it is more likely that their employees simply claim more occupational diseases. This could be either because they have better sources of information about occupational diseases, or because they perceive that this strategy increases the likelihood of a successful claim. It will be shown later that the method of resolution of litigated cases is also associated with the type of claim. Those claims that allege some occupational disease are much more likely to be redeemed than those that involve personal injuries only.

One element of litigated cases that is concrete is the timing of the injury or injuries claimed. Table 3-20 shows the year of the last reported injury for this sample of closed litigated cases. A majority of the cases had a last reported injury in 1976 or 1977. But the most interesting feature of table 3-20 is the tail of the distribution. Nearly 45 percent of these cases closed in late 1978 reported that the last injury occurred in 1975 or earlier. Nor does this reflect a long period of weekly benefit payments before closure; most of these cases had their hearings during 1978, primarily in July and August. This table offers some insight into the magnitude of the delays attendant upon the litigation process in Michigan. This subject will be covered in more detail in the next chapter. For the purpose of describing the litigated case population in Michigan, it is sufficient to point out that these cases and the injuries involved in them are old when they are adjudicated and even older when they are closed.

Table 3-21 demonstrates that not all litigated cases actually come to a hearing. In fact, nearly 22 percent of the closed cases in the MCCS sample did not. The categories in table 3-21 need some explanation for an understanding of the

Table 3-20
Year of Last Reported Injury Litigated Cases

Year	Number of cases	Percent
Pre-1968	23	1.9
1968	15	1.3
1969	16	1.3
1970	27	2.3
1971	27	2.3
1972	35	2.9
1973	69	5.8
1974	119	10.0
1975	182	15.3
1976	357	30.0
1977	300	25.2
1978	19	1.6
Total	1,189	100.0
Missing cases	35	
Grand total	1,224	

Column may not add to total due to rounding.

litigation process in Michigan. The "claim accepted" cases are those where the insurer decided to begin weekly payments to the claimant before the actual date of the hearing, thus validating the claim. This could be due to the emergence of evidence during the preparation for hearing, the arguments of the claimant's attorney at the pre-trial conference, a change in the circumstances of the case, or the intervention of the Bureau of Workers' Disability Compensation. Through this route some 3.4 percent of litigated cases essentially revert to unlitigated status and receive the benefits they would have been entitled to in the first place.

An additional group of 5.2 percent of cases are "dismissed" for lack of prosecution or various technical flaws. Most of these are cases where the claimant, or the claimant's at-

Table 3-21
Hearing Status by Insurer Type

Hearing status	Total		Carrier		Insurer type Big three		Other self-insurers	
	Number	Percent	Number	Percent	Number	Percent	Number	Percent
Hearing held	919	78.3	453	78.5	312	78.4	154	77.4
Claim accepted	40	3.4	23	4.0	9	2.3	8	4.0
Claim dismissed	61	5.2	25	4.3	28	7.0	8	4.0
Claim withdrawn	154	13.1	76	13.2	49	12.3	29	14.6
Total	1,174	100.0	577	100.0	398	100.0	199	100.0
Missing cases	50							
Grand total	1,224							

Chi-square (unweighted) = 6.81 with 6 degrees of freedom.
Columns may not add to total due to rounding.

torney, does not show up or fails to respond at one of the required administrative stages in the litigation process. These cases essentially are dropouts from the litigation system and, presumably, are not seen again. The "withdrawn" category is somewhat different in that the petitioner, usually the employee, decides to terminate the litigation procedure before it comes to a hearing. Some of these cases will find their way back into the system again at some future date. Thus calling these cases "closed" may be somewhat premature.

Table 3-22 shows the outcome for the 78 percent of litigated cases that do come to a hearing. More than 90 percent of the hearings for the cases in this sample were redemption hearings, and 99 percent of these were approved (831 out of 837). It is obvious that the typical compensated litigated case is a lump-sum redemption. This is the basis of the judgment that Michigan really operates a two-tiered workers' compensation system. The wage-loss principle organizes the unlitigated system, while the litigated system is dominated by compromise and release settlements.

The other outcomes identified in table 3-22 generally involve weekly benefit payments rather than lump-sums. The "benefits awarded" and "benefits denied" categories represent the hearing officers' decisions in cases that are litigated to conclusion. According to the MCCS, about 3.1 percent and 1.4 percent, respectively, of litigated cases fall into these categories.[4]

Another 1.4 percent of litigated cases are "accepted" by the insurer during the hearing itself. This is in addition to the 3.4 percent accepted prior to the hearing. Thus about 5 percent of all litigated cases are finally accepted by the insurer. There is also a small group of about 2 percent of litigated cases that are labeled "stipulations." These are basically judges' awards that the parties have jointly agreed upon, therefore no appeal is to be expected in these cases. It is in-

Table 3-22
Outcome of Hearing by Insurer Type

Outcome of hearing	Total		Insurer type					
			Carrier		Big three		Other self-insurers	
	Number	Percent	Number	Percent	Number	Percent	Number	Percent
Redemption approved	831	90.1	410	89.9	283	90.7	138	89.6
Redemption denied	6	0.7	3	0.7	1	0.3	2	1.3
Benefits awarded	29	3.1	10	2.2	13	4.2	6	3.9
Benefits denied	13	1.4	7	1.5	5	1.6	1	0.6
Claim accepted	13	1.4	8	1.8	3	1.0	2	1.3
Stipulation	18	2.0	15	3.3	1	0.3	2	1.3
Advance approved	1	0.1	0	0.0	1	0.3	0	0.0
Other	11	1.2	3	0.7	5	1.6	3	1.9
Total	922	100.0	456	100.0	312	100.0	154	100.0
Missing cases	302							
Grand total	1,224							

Chi-square (unweighted) = 18.76 with 14 degrees of freedom.
Columns may not add to total due to rounding.

teresting to note that there is no statistically significant difference among the three insurer types in the outcomes of hearings in their litigated cases. This result was observed in table 3-21 as well. The conclusion is that while there are considerable differences in the proportion of cases litigated, there are no significant differences in the types of outcomes observed for the three types of insurers.

This is borne out again in table 3-23, Appeal Status by Insurer Type. Approximately 5 percent of all litigated cases are eventually appealed, with roughly an equal number of appeals coming from the employees and the insurers. This table indicates that the likelihood of appeal is not related to the type of insurer. It also seriously understates the importance of the appeals process by relating the number of appeals to the total litigated case population. Table 3-24 reveals that most of the appeals come from cases involving judges' opinions, as would be expected. Only about 2 percent of redemption settlements in the sample involved the appeals process (and of course the appeal could possibly have preceded the redemption). But *over half* of the judges' decisions were appealed, with 24 percent appealed by the employee and 28 percent appealed by the insurer.

When the appeals results are presented in this way, the picture is very revealing. Only 5 percent of litigated cases are appealed, but these cases constitute 50 percent of the judges' decisions. This would seem to raise some serious questions about the adjudicative process in Michigan workers' compensation. Ninety percent of the hearings are to approve redemptions. Only 1 percent of these are disapproved, so there is some question as to exactly what has been accomplished. Of the remaining 10 percent of the hearings, half are appealed anyway. This raises serious questions about the efficacy of the hearings procedure. It is difficult to see what has been gained by this administrative treatment, other than delay.

Table 3-23
Appeals Status by Insurer Type

| Appeals status | Total | | Insurer type | | | | | | |
| | | | Carrier | | Big three | | Other self-insurers | |
	Number	Percent	Number	Percent	Number	Percent	Number	Percent
Not appealed	1,109	94.7	549	95.3	373	94.4	187	93.5
Appealed by employee	32	2.7	12	2.1	12	3.0	8	4.0
Appealed by insurer	30	2.6	15	2.6	10	2.5	5	2.5
Total	1,171	100.0	576	100.0	395	100.0	200	100.0
Missing cases	53							
Grand total	1,224							

Chi-square (unweighted) = 2.26 with 4 degrees of freedom.
Columns may not add to total due to rounding.

Table 3-24
Appeal Status by Method of Resolution

							Resolution						
	Total		Redeemed		Withdrawn		Dismissed		Accepted		Decision	
Appeal status	Number	Percent	Number	Percent	Number	Percent	Number	Percent	Number	Percent	Number	Percent
Not appealed	1,148	94.6	832	97.8	163	99.4	61	93.8	56	94.9	36	48.0
Appealed by employee	32	2.6	8	0.9	0	0.0	4	6.2	2	3.4	18	24.0
Appealed by insurer	34	2.8	11	1.3	1	0.6	0	0.0	1	1.7	21	28.0
Total	1,214	100.0	851	100.0	164	100.0	65	100.0	59	100.0	75	100.0
Missing cases	10											
Grand total	1,224											

Chi-square = 347.03** with 8 degrees of freedom.
Columns may not add to total due to rounding.

The final element of this description of the litigation process will be the method of resolution. In essence, this represents a summary version of tables 3-21 and 3-22 since it combines the outcomes, ignoring the question of whether a hearing actually took place. Table 3-25 indicates that about 70 percent of all litigated cases end up as redemption settlements. About 6 percent actually require a judge's opinion, either award or denial. Roughly 5 percent are accepted by the insurer somewhere along the litigation process; a similar number are dismissed by the law judge for various reasons. This leaves a group of about 13 percent of all litigated cases that are withdrawn by the petitioner before conclusion. While there are minor variations in these proportions among the insurer types, they are not significant. Therefore the conclusion, based on the evidence of the MCCS, is that the resolution of litigated cases does not vary across insurer types.

It does vary systematically with some other case characteristics, however. Table 3-26 shows that the method of resolution differs substantially with the type of injury. In particular, cases that involve claims of occupational disease, either alone or in concert with personal injury, have a markedly higher incidence of redemption settlements. Litigated cases that involve an occupational disease claim are redeemed nearly 80 percent of the time, whereas litigated personal injury cases are only redeemed about 60 percent of the time. Claims of occupational disease are also accepted by the insurer less often than are personal injury cases. Contrarily, the number of "washouts" seems to be less in occupational disease claims. Table 3-26 reveals that over 25 percent of personal injury cases are withdrawn or dismissed; this compares with only about 14 percent of cases alleging occupational disease. The reasons for these differences are not obvious, but it was shown in table 3-25 that there were no substantial differences by insurer type, so that factor does not offer a satisfactory explanation.

Table 3-25
Case Resolution by Insurer Type

| Case resolution | Total | | Insurer type | | | | | |
| | | | Carrier | | Big three | | Other self-insurers | |
	Number	Percent	Number	Percent	Number	Percent	Number	Percent
Redeemed	836	70.9	412	71.2	284	71.4	140	69.3
Withdrawn	154	13.1	74	12.8	50	12.6	30	14.9
Dismissed	59	5.0	23	4.0	28	7.0	8	4.0
Accepted	59	5.0	34	5.9	13	3.3	12	5.9
Decision	71	6.0	36	6.2	23	5.8	12	5.9
Total	1,179	100.0	579	100.0	398	100.0	202	100.0
Missing cases	45							
Grand total	1,224							

Chi-square (unweighted) = 9.35 with 8 degrees of freedom.
Columns may not add to total due to rounding.

Table 3-26
Type of Injury by Method of Resolution

Type of injury	Total		Redeemed		Withdrawn		Resolution Dismissed		Accepted		Decision	
	Number	Percent	Number	Percent	Number	Percent	Number	Percent	Number	Percent	Number	Percent
Personal injury only	504	100.0	297	58.9	86	17.1	42	8.3	41	8.1	38	7.5
Occupational disease only	307	100.0	243	79.2	32	10.4	11	3.6	4	1.3	17	5.5
Both	389	100.0	301	77.4	46	11.8	12	3.1	11	2.8	19	4.9
Total	1,200	100.0	841	70.1	164	13.7	65	5.4	56	4.7	74	6.2
Missing cases	24											
Grand total	1,224											

Chi-square = 62.84** with 8 degrees of freedom.

Rows may not add to total due to rounding.

Table 3-27 presents the results of another linear probability regression analysis. This time the dependent variable is the conditional probability that a case is redeemed given that it is litigated. This regression equation was estimated on the litigated sample of 1,224 cases; no weighting was necessary in this instance. The list of independent variables is the same as used earlier in the chapter, except that the various injury categories are omitted. The occupational disease variable has been added as a replacement since the injury categories did not prove as useful in discriminating among litigated cases as they were in distinguishing litigated cases from unlitigated cases.

Table 3-27
Probability of Redemption for Litigated Cases
Linear Probability Regression

Dependent variable - probability of redemption given litigation
$p(REDEM | LIT) = .698$

$\bar{X}$	Independent variables	$\hat{\beta}$	se	t
.703	Detroit	-.016	.034	.46
.325	Big three	-.088	.057	1.53
.165	Other self-insurers	-.025	.036	.70
.248	Detroit and big three	.007	.062	.11
.312	Age (55 or over)	.135	.036	3.76**
.133	Age and big three	.142	.057	2.49*
.243	Female	.063	.030	2.10*
.089	Multiple spells	-.036	.046	.79
.041	Fatality	.027	.064	.43
.569	Occupational disease	.157	.027	5.81**
	Constant	.577		

n = 1,224
F(10, 1213) = 11.33**
$R^2 = .085$

There are only four coefficients in the estimated linear probability regression equation that are significantly different from zero. Claimants aged 55 and over appear to be 13.5 percent more likely to be redeemed than their younger colleagues. Older auto workers (an interaction term) are an additional 14.2 percent more likely to be redeemed, over and above the contribution of age alone. Female claimants appear to be 6.3 percent more likely to be redeemed than male claimants. And litigated cases that involve some claim of occupational disease are 15.7 percent more likely to be redeemed than if no occupational disease is claimed. As stated earlier, these four coefficients are significantly different from zero, but only these four. The insurer does not make a difference (as shown in table 3-25), Detroit origin does not make a difference, the number of earlier spells of disability does not make a difference, and fatalities do not show up as significantly different from other cases.

Perhaps the most interesting statistic in this instance is the coefficient of variation. The R^2 statistic reported in table 3-27 reveals that less than 9 percent of the variance in the probability of redemption is accounted for by the variables in the regression. Thus the most important conclusion of the regression analysis is that these factors are not very successful in explaining the variation in outcome of litigated cases. In other words, they do not shed much light on the question of which cases are redeemed.

This review of litigation in Michigan's workers' compensation system has proved to be somewhat mixed. The origins of litigated claims were described in some detail and specificity. Claims from the Detroit area, from auto workers, older workers, and those claims involving larger indemnity amounts were shown to be significantly more likely to be litigated. Fatalities and claims involving multiple injuries were also associated with litigation. Claims against self-insurers other than the big three and claims involving relatively straightforward injuries such as cuts, burns, and fractures were shown to be significantly less likely to be litigated.

The attempt to explain the outcome of litigation was less successful, however. Mostly this reflects the inadequate information available from the official record. It is clear that most litigated cases end up as redemptions. The fact that retiree claims and occupational disease claims are more likely to end up as redemptions is also of interest. The litigation process in Michigan's workers' compensation system appears from this review to function primarily as a forum for validating compromise and release agreements. Whether the resources devoted to this administrative system, or the delays introduced, are justified by these results seems to be a very relevant question in light of these findings.

NOTES

1. See chapter 1 for a fuller discussion of this procedure as it relates to the sampling design employed in this study.

2. D. R. Cox, *Analysis of Binary Data* (London: Methuen & Co., 1970), chapter 2. See also E. Malinvaud, *Statistical Methods of Econometrics* (Chicago: Rand McNally, 1966), pp. 254-8.

3. The specification implications of this question are rather unpleasant. However, in the descriptive spirit of this investigation, it does not seem appropriate to go beyond a simple analysis of variance approach to multivariate hypothesis testing.

4. But recall from chapter 1 that the MCCS sample is deficient in judges' decisions relative to other types of outcomes.

BENEFIT DELIVERY 4

Introduction

This chapter will address two major questions; what is paid in indemnity benefits to workers' compensation claimants, and how soon is it paid? Thus the thrust of the chapter is the adequacy and timeliness of the income maintenance benefits paid to claimants in the Michigan Closed Case Survey samples.

As table 4-1 indicates, it will be appropriate to distinguish between the types of payment (weekly, lump-sum, both, or none) as well as the types of case (litigated or unlitigated) in this analysis.[1] For while unlitigated cases are only paid weekly benefits (except for occasional lump-sum advances), litigated cases show a very high incidence of lump-sum payments, as discussed in chapter 3. Obviously, lump-sum payments and weekly payments require different consideration. In particular, it is not possible to calculate the proportion of lost income replaced by a lump-sum payment unless one knows the specific term of income loss. Generally, in the lump-sum cases in the sample, this is not known.

It is also somewhat misleading to compare delays in payment for litigated cases and unlitigated cases. Of course, from the point of view of the injured worker, any litigation delay may be a disaster. But according to table 4-1, 18 per-

Table 4-1
Type of Compensation by Type of Case

| Compensation type | Total | | Litigation status | | | |
| | | | Unlitigated | | Litigated | |
	Number	Percent	Number	Percent	Number	Percent
Lump-sum payment only	692	31.8	0	0.0	692	56.5
Weekly payments only	1,012	46.5	909	95.3	103	8.4
Both	207	9.5	0	0.0	207	16.9
None	267	12.3	45	4.7	222	18.1
Total	2,178	100.0	954	100.0	1,224	100.0

Chi-square = 1,650.16** with 3 degrees of freedom.
Columns may not add to total due to rounding.

cent of litigated claims are not compensated at all. Therefore, the process causing the delay did at least serve to separate the compensated from the uncompensated, even if this was primarily a claimant's decision. Whether the delay is worth it is a more difficult policy question, but at least it is clear that it is unfair to compare litigated and unlitigated cases in this regard.

One way in which litigated and unlitigated cases can be compared is in total dollars of indemnity received by the claimant. Table 4-2 presents the distribution of indemnity payments by litigation status. It is obvious that these cases have very different outcomes. The average litigated case in the sample received nearly $6,000 in indemnity compared to less than $900 for the unlitigated. Further, this average includes the litigated cases that do not receive any indemnity at all. Excluding the uncompensated cases, the litigated average would be nearly $7,500.

As was discussed at great length in chapter 1, the distribution of indemnity for weekly payment cases is biased with a closed case sampling design. The long term weekly payment cases are derived from a smaller population than the short term ones. They are also characterized by the lower weekly benefit levels representative of earlier earning levels. Even accounting for this bias, however, the contrast between the distribution of litigated and unlitigated cases is very great. Whereas less than 10 percent of unlitigated cases are paid more than $2,000 in indemnity, nearly 60 percent of litigated cases receive this amount. Less than 1 percent of unlitigated cases receive more than $8,000 in indemnity compared to over 20 percent of litigated cases.

Table 4-3 shows that this result is not a consequence of the size of the lump-sum settlements in litigated cases. Table 4-3 presents the distribution of *weekly* indemnity payments by litigation status. The category of no payments had to be

Table 4-2
Total Indemnity Received by Type of Case

Total indemnity received	Total		Type of case Unlitigated		Litigated	
	Number	Percent	Number	Percent	Number	Percent
None	277	12.7	45	4.7	232	19.0
$1 - $125	237	10.9	208	21.8	29	2.4
$126 - $250	65	3.0	53	5.6	12	1.0
$251 - $500	245	11.2	221	23.2	24	2.0
$501 - $1,000	251	11.5	195	20.4	56	4.6
$1,001 - $2,000	300	13.8	138	14.5	162	13.2
$2,001 - $4,000	305	14.0	63	6.6	242	19.8
$4,001 - $8,000	220	10.1	24	2.5	196	16.0
$8,001 - $16,000	150	6.9	4	0.4	146	11.9
$16,001 - $32,000	95	4.4	3	0.3	92	7.5
Over $32,000	33	1.5	0	0.0	33	2.7
Total	2,178	100.0	954	100.0	1,224	100.0
Missing cases	0		$\bar{X} = \$876$		$\bar{X} = \$5,942$	
Grand total	2,178					

Chi-square = 996.78** with 10 degrees of freedom.
Columns may not add to total due to rounding.

Table 4-3
Total Weekly Compensation Paid by Type of Case

Total weekly compensation paid	Total		Type of case			
			Unlitigated		Litigated	
	Number	Percent	Number	Percent	Number	Percent
$1 - $125	218	17.9	208	22.9	10	3.2
$126 - $250	62	5.1	53	5.8	9	2.9
$251 - $500	256	21.0	221	24.3	35	11.3
$501 - $1,000	230	18.9	195	21.5	35	11.3
$1,001 - $2,000	193	15.8	138	15.2	55	17.7
$2,001 - $4,000	108	8.9	63	6.9	45	14.5
$4,001 - $8,000	64	5.3	24	2.6	40	12.9
$8,001 - $16,000	47	3.9	4	0.4	43	13.9
Over $16,000	41	3.4	3	0.3	38	12.3
Total	1,219	100.0	909	100.0	310	100.0
Missing cases	959		$\bar{X} = \$919$		$\bar{X} = \$6,423$	
Grand total	2,178					

Chi-square = 353.44** with 8 degrees of freedom.
Columns may not add to total due to rounding.

eliminated from this table since it would swamp the results for the litigated sample, so the averages are not consistent with table 4-2. Table 4-3 shows that the mixture of payment types in table 4-2 did not distort the comparison between litigated and unlitigated cases. The litigated cases are much more expensive, whether measured in terms of total indemnity or weekly payments only. What these measures cannot show is whether the cases are more expensive because they are litigated or whether they are litigated because they are more expensive. As discussed earlier, the MCCS data base is not sufficient to answer this critical question. Building on this judgment that litigated and unlitigated cases are very different, the analysis proceeds with the discussion of compensation payments to unlitigated cases.

What Is Paid to Unlitigated Cases

Table 4-4 indicates the weekly compensation rate for unlitigated cases in the MCCS. As is shown in the table, two-thirds of all weekly payment cases received between $100 and $150 per week. The distribution of weekly compensation rates is very tight for two reasons. First, Michigan has very high minimum benefit levels. While these were never enacted by the legislature, the Michigan Court of Appeals in 1973 extended to minimum benefits the statutory provision that adjusted maximum benefit levels annually in accord with the change in the state average weekly wage.[2] The effect of shifting both minimums and maximums up by a fixed dollar amount every year has been to compress the range within which the two-thirds statutory replacement rate operates.

In 1968, the minimum benefit for a disabled worker with three dependents was $36 per week. The maximum was $81 per week, or a difference of $45 per week. As can be seen in table 4-5, the 1978 minimum for the same worker is $114 while the 1978 maximum is $159, still an absolute difference of $45. But relatively speaking, the 1968 maximum was more

Table 4-4
Initial Weekly Compensation Rate by Insurer Type
Unlitigated Cases

Initial weekly compensation rate	Total		Insurer type					
			Carrier		Big three		Other self-insurers	
	Number	Percent	Number	Percent	Number	Percent	Number	Percent
$1 - $50	26	2.9	24	4.4	0	0.0	2	0.8
$51 - $100	21	2.3	14	2.6	2	1.7	5	2.1
$101 - $150	608	67.3	386	71.0	63	52.1	159	66.8
$151 - $200	248	27.5	120	22.1	56	46.3	72	30.3
Total	903	100.0	544	100.0	121	100.0	238	100.0
			$\bar{X} = \$129$		$\bar{X} = \$149$		$\bar{X} = \$141$	
Missing cases	51							
Grand total	954							

Chi-square = 39.11** with 6 degrees of freedom.
Columns may not add to total due to rounding.

Table 4-5
Minimum and Maximum Benefit Levels in 1978

Dependents	Weekly benefit levels	
	Minimum	Maximum
0	105	142
1	108	147
2	111	153
3	114	159
4	117	165
5 or more	120	171

SOURCE: Bureau of Workers' Disability Compensation, Michigan Department of Labor.

than twice the minimum, while the 1978 maximum is only 40 percent greater than the minimum. So the range is considerably reduced and a greater proportion of weekly benefit rates are compressed into a narrow interval.

The other element of Michigan law that served to compress the weekly compensation rate distribution was the so-called 25-hour rule. The statute (Sec. 418.371) specified that the workers' compensation weekly benefit should be based on at least 40 times the hourly earnings, unless the employee was employed "specifically and not temporarily on a part-time basis." In that event, the weekly earnings would be determined by multiplying the average wage rate by the normal hours. However, the statute went on to specify that if the employee worked an average of 25 hours per week or more, the 40-hour earnings rate should apply. In other words, the statute arbitrarily increased the compensation rate for those working more than 25 but less than 40 hours per week. This factor would also tend to compress the range of observed weekly benefit rates.

Table 4-4 demonstrated that the three insurer types (carrier, big three, and other self-insurers) have different weekly compensation levels. This point is made even more clearly by table 4-6 which shows the proportion of weekly benefit payments at the minimum, the maximum, or in between. This table is also an improvement over table 4-4 in that for each injury year, the actual weekly benefit paid is tested against the schedule in effect for that year, thus eliminating the bias introduced by the time trend in benefit levels. Table 4-6 shows that all of the big three, 74 percent of other self-insurer, and 52 percent of carrier cases are compensated at the maximum.

On the other hand, 22 percent of carrier claims get the minimum benefit along with 9 percent of other self-insurer cases. This leaves a remainder of only one-fifth of all cases that actually receive the statutory two-thirds replacement of gross earnings when they are disabled. This is a most dramatic illustration of the impact of the maximum and minimum benefit structure in Michigan. Only a small minority of injured workers actually receive the specified replacement rate.

Table 4-7 reports the weekly income replacement rate calculated from the data in the official record of each case. The actual weekly compensation rate paid is divided by the employer-reported gross weekly earnings to determine the weekly wage replacement rate. There are a number of interesting features to this table. In the first place, it demonstrates that over 4 percent of insurance carrier beneficiaries are receiving more than 100 percent wage replacement, i.e., they are getting more in tax-exempt workers' compensation benefits than they earned in pre-tax dollars before their injury. This reflects the operation of the minimum benefit level and the 25-hour rule reported earlier.

Over two-thirds of big three claimants are receiving less than 50 percent replacement of lost earnings. Nearly half the claimants from other self-insurers find themselves in the

Table 4-6
Benefit Rate by Insurer Type
Unlitigated Cases

| Benefit rate | Total | | Insurer type | | | | | |
| | | | Carrier | | Big three | | Other self-insurers | |
	Number	Percent	Number	Percent	Number	Percent	Number	Percent
Minimum benefit	142	15.8	121	22.4	0	0.0	21	8.9
Two-thirds of wage	177	19.8	137	25.4	0	0.0	40	16.9
Maximum benefit	577	64.4	281	52.1	121	100.0	175	74.2
Total	896	100.0	539	100.0	121	100.0	236	100.0
Missing cases	58							
Grand total	954							

Chi-square = 114.67** with 4 degrees of freedom.
Columns may not add to total due to rounding.

Table 4-7
Replacement Rate by Insurer Type
Unlitigated Cases

Replacement rate					Insurer type					
	Total		Carrier		Big three		Other self-insurers			
	Number	Percent	Number	Percent	Number	Percent	Number	Percent		
Up to 40%	131	14.7	73	13.5	25	21.0	33	14.3		
40% to 50%	184	20.7	72	13.3	57	47.9	55	23.8		
50% to 60%	146	16.4	72	13.3	27	22.7	47	20.3		
60% to 70%	315	35.4	232	42.9	4	3.4	79	34.2		
70% to 100%	90	10.1	68	12.6	6	5.0	16	6.9		
Over 100%	25	2.8	24	4.4	0	0.0	1	0.4		
Total	891	100.0	541	100.0	119	100.0	231	100.0		
Missing cases	63									
Grand total	954									

Chi-square = 134.93** with 10 degrees of freedom.
Columns may not add to total due to rounding.

same situation, as do one-fourth of carrier claimants. Obviously, the operation of the Michigan benefit formula combined with the wage differences in the state has produced some strange results. Some people, especially low-wage workers and part-time employees, are being compensated considerably above the statutory rate while the high-wage earners or those with fewer dependents are compensated at lower rates relative to their earnings.

The effect of the wage level on the replacement rate can be seen in table 4-8. It shows that as reported weekly earnings rise, the replacement rate declines. Workers earning over $400 per week at the time of disablement all received less than 50 percent replacement, because of the maximum benefit limitation. For workers earning less than $100 per week before injury, one-third experience more than 100 percent weekly income loss replacement due to the operation of the minimum benefit and the 25-hour rule.[3]

Turning from the weekly benefit amount to the other major variant in weekly benefit cases, the duration of payment, table 4-9 shows durations by insurer type. It should be reiterated that there is a bias in table 4-9, introduced by the closed case sampling design, that causes long duration cases to be underrepresented. So the distribution shown in table 4-9 is not perfectly representative of the durations experienced under a policy year format.[4] Nevertheless, these results do convey the essence of the duration distribution. There are a great many short duration disabilities, and relatively few long duration disabilities among the unlitigated case population.

As shown in the table, about one-fifth of the compensated cases (uncompensated cases are not included in table 4-9) have durations of one week or less. Less than 2 percent of closed unlitigated cases show durations greater than one year. Furthermore, table 4-9 indicates that while there are

Table 4-8
Replacement Rate by Weekly Earnings
Unlitigated Cases

Replacement rate					Weekly earnings							
	Total		To $100		$101-$200		$201-$300		$301-$400		Over $400	
	Number	Percent	Number	Percent	Number	Percent	Number	Percent	Number	Percent	Number	Percent
Up to 40%	131	14.6	1	2.3	0	0.0	2	0.6	28	14.9	100	95.0
40% to 50%	184	20.5	0	0.0	1	0.4	40	12.5	138	73.4	5	5.0
50% to 60%	148	16.5	0	0.0	3	1.3	123	38.3	22	11.7	0	0.0
60% to 70%	318	35.5	28	65.1	138	57.7	152	47.4	0	0.0	0	0.0
70% to 100%	90	10.0	0	0.0	86	36.0	4	1.2	0	0.0	0	0.0
Over 100%	25	2.8	14	32.6	11	4.6	0	0.0	0	0.0	0	0.0
Total	896	100.0	43	100.0	239	100.0	321	100.0	188	100.0	105	100.0
Missing cases	58											
Grand total	954											

Chi-square = 1,574.15** with 25 degrees of freedom.

Columns may not add to total due to rounding.

Table 4-9
Duration of Weekly Compensation Payments by Insurer Type
Unlitigated Cases

Duration of weekly compensation payments	Total		Insurer type					
			Carrier		Big three		Other self-insurers	
	Number	Percent	Number	Percent	Number	Percent	Number	Percent
Up to 1 week	204	22.7	136	25.3	23	19.0	45	18.9
1 to 2 weeks	64	7.1	38	7.1	11	9.1	15	6.3
2 to 4 weeks	234	26.1	137	25.5	33	27.3	64	26.9
4 to 8 weeks	205	22.9	120	22.3	26	21.5	59	24.8
8 to 13 weeks	85	9.5	53	9.9	10	8.3	22	9.2
13 to 26 weeks	69	7.7	35	6.5	11	9.1	23	9.7
26 to 52 weeks	23	2.6	11	2.0	5	4.1	7	2.9
1 to 2 years	9	1.0	4	0.7	2	1.7	3	1.3
2 to 4 years	3	0.3	3	0.6	0	0.0	0	0.0
Over 4 years	1	0.1	1	0.2	0	0.0	0	0.0
Total	897	100.0	538	100.0	121	100.0	238	100.0
Missing cases	57		$\bar{X} = 7.1$		$\bar{X} = 7.5$		$\bar{X} = 6.7$	
Grand total	954							

Chi-square = 13.78 with 18 degrees of freedom.
Columns may not add to total due to rounding.

slight differences in the average duration of unlitigated cases by type of insurer, these differences are not statistically significant.

There is another interesting element in table 4-9, and that is the dearth of one- to two-week duration cases. This results from the combination of the one-week waiting period before workers' compensation benefits begin and a two-week disability trigger for retroactive payment for the first week. In other words, if a worker is disabled and misses work for one week or less, he or she receives no compensation. Compensation begins on the eighth day after the injury. But if the disability extends another full week, then payment is made for the first week as well.

Logically, therefore, disabled workers should be paid either for one week (or less) or for more than two weeks, since the extra week is triggered with the first day of the second compensated week. This point is demonstrated in table 4-10, which breaks the first four weeks of duration down into greater detail. It is clear that the bulk of the one- to two-week duration cases are paid for exactly two weeks (14 days). Presumably the 15 cases that were paid more than one week but less than two weeks are either voluntary additional payments by insurers, errors in payment or errors in measurement of the payments.

Table 4-10 also speaks to those who argue that the potential reimbursement of the first week induces disabled workers to stay off the job longer than otherwise necessary. There is no sure way to determine when a worker could have returned to work, especially from the written record of a workers' compensation case. What can be observed is the behavioral result, namely, continued absence from work and qualification for additional days of compensation. In table 4-10 this would be apparent in a declining number of cases as the trigger duration is approached and the reappearance of these cases on or just after the trigger point.

Table 4-10
Duration Detail for Short Term Unlitigated Cases

Duration	Number of short term unlitigated cases
Up to 1 week	
1 day	38
2 days	51
3 days	41
4 days	38
5 days	37
1 to 2 weeks	
8-13 days	15
14 days	49
2 to 4 weeks	
15 days	30
16 days	31
17 days	22
18 days	28
19 days	11
21 days	25
22 days	19
23 days	13
24 days	9
25 days	12
26 days	13
28 days	22

In the case of Michigan workers' compensation system, one would expect to find a declining number of cases as the duration of compensation nears one full week (two weeks of disability). This would be offset by a larger number of cases that were paid exactly two weeks of disability benefits. According to the evidence in table 4-10, this is a relatively minor problem. There were 37 cases with five days duration, 49 cases with 14 days and 30 cases with 15 days. Further, the general shape of the duration distribution is quite smooth and regular; there is no enormous peak at the trigger duration. It is quite possible that workers are not well enough informed about their rights under the workers' compensation statute to play this retroactive compensation game. But the conclusion is that this is not a serious problem at the present time.

The product of the duration of payment (in weeks) and the weekly benefit amount is the total weekly compensation paid. This figure is reported in table 4-11 for unlitigated cases by insurer type. The distribution is quite similar to that of table 4-9 since the major variation is in duration. It is noteworthy that approximately three-fourths of the unlitigated weekly benefit cases involve less than $1,000 in total indemnity. Once again there is no significant difference by insurer type, even though the means do tend to parallel the wage and benefit levels reported earlier.

What Is Paid to Litigated Cases

Because of the wide diversity in the litigated case population, it seems advisable to proceed with a disaggregated description. First a few characterizations of lump-sum as opposed to weekly benefit cases will be offered. Then the discussion will proceed with a description of weekly benefit cases. This will be followed by an examination of what is known about lump-sum payment cases. The final section will attempt to pull these disparate elements back together with a discussion of the total indemnity paid to litigated cases.

Table 4-12 reports the relationship between the final resolution of the case and the type of compensation paid. This should be helpful in establishing a general feel for the types of cases represented in the lump-sum payment and weekly payment groups. As would be expected, redeemed cases all show lump-sum payments. About 20 percent of the redemptions also received weekly benefit payments; generally, this was during an earlier period of disability. The cases

Table 4-11
Total Weekly Compensation Paid by Insurer Type
Unlitigated Cases

| Total weekly compensation paid | Total | | Insurer type | | | | | |
| | | | Carrier | | Big three | | Other self-insurers | |
	Number	Percent	Number	Percent	Number	Percent	Number	Percent
$1 - $125	207	22.9	139	25.5	22	18.2	46	19.3
$126 - $250	53	5.9	40	7.3	3	2.5	10	4.2
$251 - $500	220	24.3	130	23.9	33	27.3	57	23.9
$501 - $1,000	192	21.2	115	21.1	24	19.8	53	22.3
$1,001 - $2,000	138	15.3	73	13.4	22	18.2	43	18.1
$2,001 - $4,000	63	7.0	32	5.9	11	9.1	20	8.4
$4,001 - $8,000	24	2.7	11	2.0	5	4.1	8	3.4
$8,001 - $16,000	4	0.4	2	0.4	1	0.8	1	0.4
Over $16,000	3	0.3	3	0.6	0	0.0	0	0.0
Total	904	100.0	545	100.0	121	100.0	238	100.0
Missing cases	50		$\bar{X} = \$885$		$\bar{X} = \$1,044$		$\bar{X} = \$940$	
Grand total	954							

Chi-square = 20.66 with 16 degrees of freedom.
Columns may not add to total due to rounding.

Table 4-12
Resolution by Type of Compensation
Litigated Cases

Resolution	Total		Type of compensation							
			Lump-sum only		Weekly only		Both		None	
	Number	Percent	Number	Percent	Number	Percent	Number	Percent	Number	Percent
Redeemed	850	100.0	664	78.1	0	0.0	186	21.9	0	0.0
Withdrawn	165	100.0	0	0.0	29	17.6	0	0.0	136	82.4
Dismissed	62	100.0	0	0.0	9	14.5	0	0.0	53	85.5
Accepted	49	100.0	8	16.3	40	81.6	1	2.0	0	0.0
Decision	71	100.0	20	28.2	24	33.8	21	29.6	6	8.5
Total	1,197	100.0	692	57.8	102	8.5	208	17.4	195	16.3
Missing cases	27									
Grand total	1,224									

Chi-square = 1,505.2** with 12 degrees of freedom.

Rows may not add to total due to rounding.

that were withdrawn or dismissed either received no payment at all (over 80 percent) or weekly payments only; again, this would usually reflect a period of disability before the application for hearing. The cases accepted by the insurer after the commencement of the litigation process tend to resemble the unlitigated cases described earlier. Less than 20 percent of these show any lump-sum payment.

The greatest variety in type of compensation occurs in the decision category. This reflects both the amount of discretion the administrative law judges possess and the complicated nature of the cases that finally require a hearing officer's determination. It should also be pointed out that there are probably more than 8.5 percent of the decisions that result in no award for the claimant. But since no distinction is made in table 4-12 between weekly compensation paid before the litigation and that paid after resolution, some cases that did not receive awards will fall into the weekly payment category by virtue of their earlier experience.

Table 4-13 looks at the question of type of compensation in a different way. It asks whether the type of compensation is influenced by whether the case originated from an occupational disease claim, a personal injury claim, or a claim asserting disability from both sources. As was shown in chapter 3, the table indicates that lump-sum payments (resulting from redemption agreements) are more prevalent in occupational disease claims. In fact, table 4-13 demonstrates that only about 5 percent of litigated occupational disease claims ever received any weekly compensation. This rises to 20 percent if the occupational disease is coupled with a personal injury claim.

The conclusion seems clear that there is something very different about the occupational disease claims. Unfortunately, it is not possible with the MCCS data base to accurately enumerate the occupational disease claims among the unlitigated cases, so it cannot be determined whether an

Table 4-13
Type of Injury by Type of Compensation

| Type of injury | Total | | Type of compensation | | | | | | | |
| | | | Lump-sum only | | Weekly only | | Both | | None | |
	Number	Percent	Number	Percent	Number	Percent	Number	Percent	Number	Percent
Personal injury only	490	100.0	187	38.2	72	14.7	135	27.6	96	19.6
Occupational disease only	301	100.0	242	80.4	8	2.7	8	2.7	43	14.3
Both	383	100.0	250	65.3	20	5.2	62	16.2	51	13.3
Total	1,174	100.0	679	57.8	100	8.5	205	17.5	190	16.2
Missing cases	50									
Grand total	1,224									

Chi-square = 174.74** with 6 degrees of freedom.
Rows may not add to total due to rounding.

unusual proportion of *all* occupational disease claims end up as redemptions. It is certainly indicative of problems in obtaining compensation for occupational disease claims, however.[5] In this regard it should be noted that the proportion of uncompensated litigated cases is actually slightly lower for the occupational disease group, so there is no evidence that these claims are "less worthy" as a group than personal injury claims. The problem of securing compensation for occupational disease claims may be very real, but the present evidence is not sufficient to make any definitive statement. All that can be said is that they are compensated differently when litigated.

Table 4-14 returns the discussion to familiar ground; it reports the type of compensation payment by insurer type for litigated cases. According to the chi-square statistic, there is a significant difference among the insurer types in the form of their compensation payments. Workers' compensation cases at the big three auto producers are significantly more likely to receive lump-sum payments only. They are much less likely to have received weekly payments at any time.

The major impact of table 4-14 is in demonstrating the overall dominance of the lump-sum payment in Michigan's workers' compensation dispute settlement system. It is frequently argued that without the redemption and the lump-sum payment, the hearings process would be hopelessly clogged with cases. Whether this is a justification or simply an apology for redemption settlements remains to be seen. But it is clear from the evidence presented in this monograph that litigation in Michigan workers' compensation system leads primarily to compromise and release settlements and lump-sum payments. Nevertheless, the weekly benefit payments to litigated workers' compensation cases will be explored first. Following this discussion, attention will return to a quantitative analysis of the lump-sum question.

Table 4-14
Type of Compensation by Insurer Type
Litigated Cases

Compensation type	Total		Insurer type					
			Carrier		Big three		Other self-insurers	
	Number	Percent	Number	Percent	Number	Percent	Number	Percent
Lump-sum payment only	677	57.4	293	50.6	270	67.8	114	56.4
Weekly payments only	100	8.5	60	10.4	22	5.5	18	8.9
Both	202	17.1	140	24.2	23	5.8	39	19.3
None	200	17.0	86	14.9	83	20.9	31	15.3
Total	1,179	100.0	579	100.0	398	100.0	202	100.0
Missing cases	45							
Grand total	1,224							

Chi-square = 71.46** with 6 degrees of freedom.
Columns may not add to total due to rounding.

The weekly benefit payments to litigated cases largely parallel the payments to unlitigated cases discussed earlier. Table 4-15 demonstrates that the same general picture emerges as in table 4-6. The bulk of the big three cases earn the maximum weekly benefit, while this is true for only about half the carrier cases. In general, the minimum benefit is only significant for the carrier segment as very few self-insurer cases involve the minimum benefit. For litigated cases, almost 30 percent are compensated at two-thirds of the gross wage compared to 20 percent of unlitigated. This would reflect the fact that litigated cases are considerably older on the average and thus do not show the same narrowing of the effective range of the benefit formula as more recent cases.

Table 4-16 compares the durations of weekly compensation payments to litigated cases by insurer type. In this instance, the contrast with the unlitigated results must be emphasized. Whereas nearly 80 percent of unlitigated cases showed durations of less than eight weeks at closure, only about 25 percent of litigated cases fall below this level. On the other hand, while only 4 percent of unlitigated closed cases had durations of more than 26 weeks, table 4-16 demonstrates that nearly half of the closed litigated cases exceeded this duration. It would seem that those litigated cases that do involve weekly compensation payments are considerably more serious disabilities than are the unlitigated cases.

The last table dealing with weekly payments to litigated cases is table 4-17. It shows the distribution of total weekly payments to litigated cases by insurer type. It parallels table 4-11 which reported the same information for unlitigated cases. As with the duration of payments, the litigated cases are revealed to be much more serious. The average amount of weekly compensation payments to litigated cases is nearly seven times that to unlitigated, even though the weekly com-

Table 4-15
Benefit Rate by Insurer Type
Litigated Cases

| Benefit rate | Total | | Insurer type | | | | | |
| | | | Carrier | | Big three | | Other self-insurers | |
	Number	Percent	Number	Percent	Number	Percent	Number	Percent
Minimum benefit	37	12.4	33	16.8	0	0.0	4	6.9
Two-thirds of wage	85	28.5	60	30.6	8	18.2	17	29.3
Maximum benefit	176	59.1	103	52.6	36	81.8	37	63.8
Total	298	100.0	196	100.0	44	100.0	58	100.0
Missing cases	926							
Grand total	1,224							

Chi-square = 17.42* with 4 degrees of freedom.
Columns may not add to total due to rounding.

Table 4-16
Duration of Weekly Compensation Payments by Insurer Type
Litigated Cases

Duration of weekly compensation payments	Total		Insurer type					
			Carrier		Big three		Other self-insurers	
	Number	Percent	Number	Percent	Number	Percent	Number	Percent
Up to 1 week	10	3.3	6	3.0	2	4.4	2	3.5
1 to 2 weeks	5	1.7	4	2.0	1	2.2	0	0.0
2 to 4 weeks	22	7.4	11	5.6	4	8.9	7	12.3
4 to 8 weeks	41	13.7	26	13.2	6	13.3	9	15.8
8 to 13 weeks	31	10.4	20	10.2	6	13.3	5	8.8
13 to 26 weeks	43	14.4	33	16.8	5	11.1	5	8.8
26 to 52 weeks	41	13.7	27	13.7	3	6.7	11	19.3
1 to 2 years	41	13.7	30	15.2	4	8.9	7	12.3
2 to 4 years	33	11.0	22	11.2	5	11.1	6	10.5
Over 4 years	32	10.7	18	9.1	9	20.0	5	8.8
Total	299	100.0	197	100.0	45	100.0	57	100.0
			$\bar{X} = 63.7$		$\bar{X} = 104.7$		$\bar{X} = 60.0$	
Missing cases	925							
Grand total	1,224							

Chi-square = 15.78 with 18 degrees of freedom.
Columns may not add to total due to rounding.

Table 4-17
Total Weekly Compensation Paid by Insurer Type
Litigated Cases

Total weekly compensation paid	Total		Insurer type					
			Carrier		Big three		Other self-insurers	
	Number	Percent	Number	Percent	Number	Percent	Number	Percent
$1 - $125	10	3.3	7	3.5	2	4.4	1	1.8
$126 - $250	9	3.0	6	3.0	2	4.4	1	1.8
$251 - $500	34	11.3	18	9.0	5	11.1	11	19.3
$501 - $1,000	34	11.3	21	10.5	7	15.6	6	10.5
$1,001 - $2,000	54	17.9	41	20.5	6	13.3	7	12.3
$2,001 - $4,000	44	14.6	33	16.5	6	13.3	5	8.8
$4,001 - $8,000	39	12.9	23	11.5	4	8.9	12	21.1
$8,001 - $16,000	41	13.6	29	14.5	5	11.1	7	12.3
Over $16,000	37	12.3	22	11.0	8	17.8	7	12.3
Total	302	100.0	200	100.0	45	100.0	57	100.0
Missing cases	922		$\bar{X} = \$6,126$		$\bar{X} = \$8,267$		$\bar{X} = \$5,677$	
Grand total	1,224							

Chi-square = 16.01 with 16 degrees of freedom.
Columns may not add to total due to rounding.

pensation rates are lower due to the vintage of the cases. As before, the highest average amount is paid by the big three, over $8,000 per case according to table 4-17. In this measurement, other self-insurers pay slightly less on the average in weekly compensation payments than do the carriers. The chi-square statistic reveals that these differences are not statistically significant, however.

Recapping the findings on weekly benefit payments to litigated cases, it was found that carriers are most likely to have made weekly payments to litigated cases, with the big three least likely. While over one-third of litigated carrier cases showed weekly payments, only 11 percent of big three cases and 28 percent of other self-insurer cases were compensated in this form. When attention was directed to the aggregate amounts of weekly compensation payments, it was found that the big three pay slightly more, primarily by virtue of a higher average weekly compensation rate.

Lump-Sum Payments to Litigated Cases

Even though the average weekly benefit payments to litigated cases that receive such payments was shown in table 4-17 to be quite high, weekly payments still constitute a small proportion of all indemnity payments ever received by closed litigated cases. This is because of the dominance of the lump-sum payments in the litigated claims resolution process in Michigan. Table 4-14 revealed that nearly 75 percent of all closed litigated cases received lump-sum payments, nearly 90 percent of compensated cases. So for practical purposes, the litigation process is a venue for bargaining over the size of lump-sum payment. Accordingly, the major interest in indemnity paid to litigated cases lies in the magnitude of the lump-sum payments.[6]

Table 4-18 shows the distribution of lump-sum payments by insurer type. There are very substantial insurer dif-

Table 4-18
Lump-Sum Payment (Gross) by Insurer Type
Litigated Cases

| Lump-sum payment | Total | | Insurer type | | | | | |
| | | | Carrier | | Big three | | Other self-insurers | |
	Number	Percent	Number	Percent	Number	Percent	Number	Percent
$1 - $1,000	49	5.6	19	4.4	20	6.8	10	6.5
$1,001 - $2,000	109	12.4	50	11.5	34	11.6	25	16.3
$2,001 - $4,000	217	24.7	85	19.6	99	33.8	33	21.6
$4,001 - $8,000	206	23.4	90	20.8	89	30.4	27	17.6
$8,001 - $16,000	153	17.4	83	19.2	37	12.6	33	21.6
$16,001 - $32,000	125	14.2	88	20.3	14	4.8	23	15.0
Over $32,000	20	2.3	18	4.2	0	0.0	2	1.3
Total	879	100.0	433	100.0	293	100.0	153	100.0
Missing cases	345		$\bar{X} = \$10,529$		$\bar{X} = \$5,659$		$\bar{X} = \$8,493$	
Grand total	1,224							

Chi-square = 78.87** with 12 degrees of freedom.
Columns may not add to total due to rounding.

ferences apparent in table 4-18, with big three lump-sum payments the smallest and carriers' the largest. One way to explain this is to cite the earlier results on the proportion of all workers' compensation cases that are litigated. It was shown in table 2-1 that the big three experienced more than double the carriers' incidence of litigation (48 percent as opposed to 22 percent of all cases), so perhaps it is not surprising to find that they pay only a little over half as much per redemption.

If a much higher incidence of litigation occurs, it may be reasonable to conclude that the "average" litigated claim is less serious in terms of the disability; or perhaps even "less worthy" as a claim. The conventional wisdom is that the big three are plagued by nuisance claims. This evidence does not contradict that hypothesis. In addition, it is suggestive that the distribution of lump-sum payments for the big three is very compact. Nearly two-thirds of big three lump-sum payments are between $2,000 and $8,000. Since only about 40 percent of payments by other insurers fall in this range, this too is consistent with a routine redemption process. Unfortunately, the quality of information about the claimed disabilities that is available in the official record does not permit a detailed examination of the actual basis of the payments.

Table 4-18 examined the size of the gross lump-sum indemnity payment by the insurer. But this is not the sum actually received by the disabled claimant; it is subject to legal and medical cost deductions. Table 4-19 shows the average legal and medical costs by insurer type, both in raw numbers and as a percentage of the gross amount received. Attorneys' fees in redemption cases are set by rule of the Director of the Bureau of Workers' Disability Compensation at not more than 15 percent on the first $25,000 and not more than 10 percent on amounts exceeding $25,000. Table 4-19 reveals that almost 16 percent of lump-sum payments do go for legal expenses; 15 percent for the attorney, and nearly 1 percent for other legal costs. There is no significant difference among the insurer types, although the dollar amounts vary with the size of the lump-sums.

Table 4-19
Legal and Medical Costs by Insurer Type
Lump-Sum Payment Cases

Legal and medical costs	Total	Insurer type		
		Carrier	Big three	Other self-insurers
Legal costs				
Mean amount	$1,314	$1,611	$911	$1,277
Proportion of award	.158	.159	.159	.157
Number of cases	831	405	285	141
Medical costs				
Mean amount	$472	$649	$372	$254
Proportion of award	.076	.079	.077	.070
Number of cases	490	215	186	89

Medical costs in redeemed cases amount to about 7.6 percent on the average, or one-half as much as the legal costs, according to table 4-19. This figure is difficult to interpret because it occasionally includes medical treatment of the claimant as well as the normal medical examination fees which would be regarded as a litigation cost rather than a medical benefit. Unfortunately, these component parts cannot be split out, so the portion of the medical costs that could appropriately be assessed as a cost of litigation rather than treatment cannot be determined. On the assumption that it is about one-half of the total, the "cost" of litigation to the claimant would be about 20 percent of the gross lump-sum settlement. Assuming that the insurer incurs a similar cost in contesting the case, the burden of litigation costs in this no-fault system is revealed to be quite high.

There is another deduction that should be made from gross lump-sum payments to arrive at the actual indemnity payment received by the claimant. As shown in table 4-20, about 18 percent of all lump-sum payment cases have a specific dollar amount reserved for future medical benefits. It is paid to the claimant as part of the lump-sum settlement, but it is intended for medical care in the future. It is difficult to determine what this actually means; some assert that it is simply a way around the social security offset against workers' compensation income maintenance benefits. According to table 4-20, all three insurer types use this device, so it is impossible to ignore it.

Table 4-20
Lump-Sum Payments Reserved for Future Medical Care
by Insurer Type

Reserves for future medical care	Total	Insurer type		
		Carrier	Big three	Other self-insurers
Number of cases	160	87	49	24
Percentage of all lump-sum cases	18.2%	20.1%	16.7%	15.7%
Average amount	$6,502	$7,188	$5,033	$7,011
Percentage of total lump-sum	.571	.477	.733	.579

As the last two rows of table 4-20 show, these payments are very sizable. On the average, they amount to nearly 60 percent of the gross lump-sum amount, somewhat more for the big three and less for carriers. Since these payments are ostensibly for medical care, and medical care benefits are excluded in all other instances in the MCCS, it is appropriate to exclude these reserved medical payments from the net lump-sums received by claimants as well.

The indemnity amounts actually received by the claimants in lump-sum settlement cases are represented in table 4-21. The same basic conclusions that were drawn from the examination of the gross lump-sums in table 4-18 apply here. The big three pay a much lower average amount, but they pay it to a larger number of cases when compared to either of the other two insurer types.

Because of the interest in the variation in size of the lump-sum payments and the serious issues raised by a compromise and release settlement system within a workers' compensation system designed to prevent litigation, a regression analysis of the lump-sum payments is presented in table 4-22. It should be interpreted carefully because the fact remains that there is no way to determine from the record of a redeemed workers' compensation case just what was the basis for the payment. But this analysis attempts to look at the question in an indirect way.

Even if the specific basis of compensation cannot be determined for a particular case, perhaps the general association of case or claimant characteristics with the size of the lump-sum settlements could offer some insight into the process. This is analogous to the statistical evidence linking cancer to smoking. While the specific process by which an individual's smoking habits contribute to his or her risk of developing lung cancer cannot be fully explained, the statistical fact that smoking and the development of lung cancer are correlated within the general population can be very useful in decision-making by both individuals and society.

The meager facts available from the MCCS about the lump-sum payment cases are correlated with the size of the net lump-sum payment to the claimant in table 4-22. Most of

Table 4-21
Net Lump-Sum Payment by Insurer Type
Litigated Cases

	Total		Insurer type					
			Carrier		Big three		Other self-insurers	
Lump-sum payment	Number	Percent	Number	Percent	Number	Percent	Number	Percent
$1 - $1,000	97	11.2	34	8.0	43	14.8	20	13.4
$1,001 - $2,000	146	16.8	68	15.9	50	17.2	28	18.8
$2,001 - $4,000	222	25.6	91	21.3	100	34.4	31	20.8
$4,001 - $8,000	195	22.5	97	22.7	68	23.4	30	20.1
$8,001 - $16,000	139	16.0	88	20.6	25	8.6	26	17.4
Over $16,000	68	7.8	49	11.5	5	1.7	14	9.4
Total	867	100.0	427	100.0	291	100.0	149	100.0
			$\bar{X} = \$7,336$		$\bar{X} = \$3,777$		$\bar{X} = \$6,186$	
Missing cases	357							
Grand total	1,224							

Chi-square = 59.54** with 10 degrees of freedom.
Columns may not add to total due to rounding.

Table 4-22
Regression Analysis of Lump-Sum Payments

	Dependent variable - net lump-sum payment to claimant $\bar{X} = \$5962$			
$\bar{X}$	Independent variables	$\hat{\beta}$	se	t
.326	Big three	-2551.0	548.8	4.65**
.167	Other self-insurers	-1538.2	633.8	2.43*
.708	Detroit	- 961.8	504.5	1.91
.370	Age (55 or over)	- 836.3	495.7	1.69
.246	Female	279.9	553.6	.51
$232	Earnings (weekly)	11.43	2.64	4.33**
.311	Hospitalized	1554.4	487.3	3.19**
.042	Fatality	671.1	1132.3	.59
.266	Weekly compensation	3584.8	642.6	5.58**
.096	Multiple spells	2072.0	906.5	2.29*
.003	Burn	-4208.1	4178.2	1.01
.008	Cut	- 675.4	2494.1	.27
.025	Fracture	936.3	1485.9	.63
.015	Inflammation	942.7	1836.1	.51
.440	Multiple injuries	- 713.4	679.3	1.05
.123	Other injuries	523.5	1171.5	.45
.194	Back injuries	3223.0	844.2	3.82**
.570	Multiple parts	1565.2	827.6	1.89
.103	Body system	1092.4	1312.9	.83
	Constant	2456.6		

n = 718

F(21, 696) = 10.73**

$R^2 = .245$

the characteristics are entered into the regression in bivariate form, that is, they are either present or absent. Further, to avoid statistical over-determination of the system, there must be an omitted category in each instance where the full set of characteristics would exhaust the population. For example, the first independent variable listed represents the big three as the insurer in the case; the second represents other self-insurers. Each reported coefficient measures the difference that the presence of that insurer type makes, on average across the sample, when compared to the carrier group (the omitted category).

In the case of the big three, table 4-22 shows that, on the average and when controlling for all the other characteristics listed as independent variables, the big three pay $2,551 less per lump-sum payment than do carriers. Furthermore, the t-statistic reported in the right-hand column shows that this number is judged, on the the basis of the variation in the sample, to be statistically significant. Thus, one can be 99 percent sure that the big three really do pay less on the basis of the evidence of the MCCS.

The analogous conclusion for the other self-insurers is that they pay $1,538 less per case, when controlling for the other characteristics listed, than would a carrier. In this instance, the t-statistic indicates that one can be 95 percent certain that there is a difference between these two groups. It is very important to point out that this analysis does not say why the difference exists. Clearly, the specificity of the information about the cases is not very great, and it may very well be that carrier cases and self-insurer cases differ systematically in ways not measured adequately in table 4-22. That is why these results should be taken as suggestive rather than determinative.

It is worthwhile pointing out that the multivariate analysis has reduced the average difference between carrier cases and big three cases from the $3,559 shown in table 4-21 to $2,551 here. It is likely that the addition of more and better information about the particulars of the case would reduce this "unexplained" differential still more.

The Detroit variable indicates that the litigation originated in one of the five counties making up the Detroit SMSA. Since this is a binary variable, the influence of Detroit as a location is measured against the balance of the state. According to table 4-22, even though Detroit lump-sum cases receive $962 less, when controlling for the other factors listed, this is not sufficient to reject the null hypothesis that the average payment is the same. In other words, on the basis of the evidence in the MCCS, it cannot be concluded that Detroit cases receive significantly smaller payments than cases from other parts of the state.

The same is true for the binary variable called age, which represents the influence on the size of the lump-sum if the claimant is 55 or older. The age 55 and over group receives $836 less on the average, but based on the sample evidence this is not sufficient to reject the hypothesis that they are paid the same. The female variable also fails the test of statistical significance and therefore the conclusion is that men and women are treated similarly in the redemption process.

It is interesting to consider these results in combination with those reported in chapter 3 on the probability of litigation (table 3-12) and the probability of redemption given litigation (table 3-27). A Detroit origin was earlier shown to have a powerful influence on the likelihood of litigation, but not on the probability of redemption. Here it has been determined that Detroit cases are also not paid significantly less when they are redeemed. In the case of age, table 3-12 showed that claims from older workers are significantly more likely to be litigated. Further, table 3-27 demonstrated that age was one of the most powerful influences on the probability of redemption. The present analysis indicates that older workers do not receive significantly smaller settlements.

For females, an entirely different pattern has emerged. Women are no more likely than men to be involved in litigation. But once they are, table 3-27 reported that they are significantly more likely to experience a redemption than men. Table 4-22 indicates that there is no difference in the size of the redemption settlements, however. There is no easy explanation for these different patterns by demographic group.

The regression results for weekly earnings reported in table 4-22 are fortunately more understandable. The coefficient reports the average association between reported weekly earnings before disablement and the size of the lump-sum payment. It indicates that each dollar of weekly earnings produces an average of $11.43 in the redemption settlement. It is reassuring to find the coefficient is positive and significant, since the indemnity under weekly payments would tend to be proportional to the earnings level.

The rest of the variables in table 4-22 represent the nature of the injury or disability in various ways. The results indicate that the fact that the claimant was hospitalized at some point in the life of the case is associated with roughly $1,550 additional in lump-sum indemnity. If the claimant ever received weekly compensation payments in connection with the claimed disability, the coefficient for weekly compensation shows that this yields $3,585 on the average in lump-sum payment when compared to those who had never received weekly payments. Further, if there were multiple spells of weekly compensation payments, table 4-22 reports that this is worth an additional $2,072.

These results could be interpreted in a way consistent with the earlier discussion of nuisance claims. The more significant claims may be those that have demonstrated their "worth" by previously qualifying for disability benefits. These might be regarded as the cases that genuinely required litigation. The remainder, what are regarded by insurers as less worthy claims, tend to be cashed out for relatively small amounts. Thus the case variables just reported may be associated with the "worthy" claims and have large positive coefficients as a result.

The last group of variables relates specifically to the type of injury reported or the part of the body injured. These variables have been reviewed before so little attention will be paid to them here. It is surprising that they performed so poorly in this regression, given their importance in associating with the likelihood of litigation. Only the back injury variable is significant in table 4-22. According to the regression, the average back injury receives an additional $3,223 in lump-sum payments. This result would seem to contradict the conventional wisdom about nuisance claims, which might lead one to expect a negative coefficient for back injury claims. Results in chapter 3 demonstrated that back injuries are significantly more likely to be litigated, but here it is shown that they receive larger settlements. This may reflect the evidentiary problems in back injury claims.

As indicated at the beginning of this discussion, one should not try to make too much of any of these results. The regression equation only explained one-fourth of the variation in the size of lump-sums to begin with. Yet, the lack of pattern to the results discussed here is troubling. The most important conclusion is simply that the lack of information available on these redemption settlements creates a very significant barrier to understanding. There is not enough information about the cases to perceive the patterns that may be present. As a result, this analysis must be regarded as somewhat speculative.

The last task in describing the indemnity payments to litigated cases in Michigan's workers' compensation system is to bring together the weekly payments and the lump-sum indemnity payments to get the total indemnity paid. As will be shown later, not all the weekly benefits were paid after the claim was contested; but from a closed case point of view this is the most complete way to look at indemnity payments.

Table 4-23 presents these data for the litigated cases in the MCCS. The dominance of the lump-sums is very clear when table 4-23 is compared to tables 4-21 and 4-11 which reported lump-sums and weekly payment amounts, respectively. The average indemnity payments in table 4-23 are very close to those of the lump-sum results. This reflects the fact reported earlier that about 75 percent of litigated cases had received no weekly payments at all.

It is also apparent from table 4-23 that the litigation process does serve to screen out some cases. Roughly one litigated case in six comes out of the process with no compensation at all. It is possible that these cases can come around again in some instances, but the conclusion must be that the litigation process does serve to disqualify some claims. However, without better information it is not possible to reach a judgment as to the efficacy of the screening.

It is noteworthy that the differences among the three insurer types in total indemnity are statistically significant according to table 4-23. Further, it seems appropriate to question why the rank ordering of the three insurer types should be the reverse of their wage levels and weekly compensation rates. Earlier in the chapter, it was speculated that perhaps the great incidence of litigated claims in the auto industry serves in effect to depreciate the value of the claims. This explanation does not fit the other self-insured employers, however, since their incidence of litigation is lower than the carrier group.

Table 4-23
Total Indemnity Received by Insurer Type
Litigated Cases

Total indemnity received	Total		Insurer type					
			Carrier		Big three		Other self-insurers	
	Number	Percent	Number	Percent	Number	Percent	Number	Percent
None	209	17.7	89	15.4	85	21.4	35	17.3
$1 - $125	28	2.4	5	0.9	17	4.3	6	3.0
$126 - $250	12	1.0	6	1.0	2	0.5	4	2.0
$251 - $500	24	2.0	13	2.2	4	1.0	7	3.5
$501 - $1,000	55	4.7	21	3.6	24	6.0	10	5.0
$1,001 - $2,000	157	13.3	74	12.8	53	13.3	30	14.9
$2,001 - $4,000	239	20.3	103	17.8	103	25.9	33	16.3
$4,001 - $8,000	192	16.3	97	16.8	70	17.6	25	12.4
$8,001 - $16,000	141	12.0	88	15.2	26	6.5	27	13.4
$16,001 - $32,000	90	7.6	62	10.7	8	2.0	20	9.9
Over $32,000	32	2.7	21	3.6	6	1.5	5	2.5
Total	1,179	100.0	579	100.0	398	100.0	202	100.0
Missing cases	45		$\bar{X} = \$7,527$		$\bar{X} = \$3,696$		$\bar{X} = \$6,165$	
Grand total	1,224							

Chi-square = 83.29** with 20 degrees of freedom.
Columns may not add to total due to rounding.

How Soon Is It Paid

The question of timeliness of benefits is a critical one in the evaluation of an income maintenance system. Adequate benefits that do not commence promptly do not accomplish the job. This is especially true in the case of workers' compensation, since one of the reasons for the establishment of the system 70 years ago was dissatisfaction with the long delays inherent in the tort liability system. As this monograph has demonstrated, there are two very different workers' compensation systems in Michigan. The unlitigated cases are processed in a manner consistent with the original no-fault principles of workers' compensation. The litigation process in Michigan, however, is a reincarnation of tort liability with reduced monetary stakes. Because these systems are so different, they will be treated separately here. First the timeliness of payment to unlitigated cases will be assessed. Then the delays in the litigation process will be described.

Unlitigated

Table 4-24 shows the time elapsed from the injury date to the date of disablement by insurer type for unlitigated cases in the MCCS. In other words, this table addresses the question of how long it is from the injury until the worker is forced off his or her job by the consequences of that injury. While table 4-24 makes it clear that a majority of claimants are disabled immediately by their injuries, there are a surprising number of instances where this is not the case. In fact, nearly 20 percent of the time the first day of disability is reported to be more than one week after the injury. This is true for almost 30 percent of the big three cases.

This result is confirmed by table 4-25, which measures the same basic interval by a different method. Table 4-25 reports the number of days between the injury and the last day of

Table 4-24
Injury Date to Date of Disablement by Insurer Type
Unlitigated Cases

| Injury date to date of disablement | Total | | Insurer type | | | | | |
| | | | Carrier | | Big three | | Other self-insurers | |
	Number	Percent	Number	Percent	Number	Percent	Number	Percent
0 or 1 day	551	62.5	356	67.2	54	46.2	141	60.0
2 to 7 days	158	17.9	84	15.8	28	23.9	46	19.6
8 to 14 days	62	7.0	32	6.0	8	6.8	22	9.4
15 to 30 days	40	4.5	24	4.5	7	6.0	9	3.8
31 to 60 days	29	3.3	15	2.8	5	4.3	9	3.8
61 to 120 days	18	2.0	8	1.5	6	5.1	4	1.7
Over 120 days	24	2.7	11	2.1	9	7.7	4	1.7
Total	882	100.0	530	100.0	117	100.0	235	100.0
Missing cases	72							
Grand total	954							

Chi-square = 34.00** with 12 degrees of freedom.
Columns may not add to total due to rounding.

Table 4-25
Injury Date to Last Day of Work by Insurer Type

Injury date to last day of work	Total		Carrier		Insurer type Big three		Other self-insurers	
	Number	Percent	Number	Percent	Number	Percent	Number	Percent
None	563	66.7	352	70.5	65	56.5	146	63.5
1 to 7 days	161	19.1	92	18.4	17	14.8	52	22.6
8 to 14 days	35	4.1	17	3.4	7	6.1	11	4.8
15 to 30 days	33	3.9	17	3.4	8	7.0	8	3.5
31 to 60 days	20	2.4	8	1.6	6	5.2	6	2.6
61 to 120 days	17	2.0	8	1.6	5	4.3	4	1.7
Over 120 days	15	1.8	5	1.0	7	6.1	3	1.3
Total	844	100.0	499	100.0	115	100.0	230	100.0
Missing cases	110							
Grand total	954							

Chi-square = 33.90** with 12 degrees of freedom.
Columns may not add to total due to rounding.

work. In two-thirds of these unlitigated cases, the injury date was the last day of work. But that means that in one-third of the cases, the claimant continued at work after the injury. The significance of this result from the point of benefit delivery is unclear, but it is a very important observation from an analytical perspective. If a large proportion of claimants continue to work after the injury, the injury date cannot be the most useful point to regard as the origin of the case.

Accordingly, table 4-26 reports the difference between the last day of work and the date of the first compensation payment for unlitigated cases by insurer type. Since the first seven days of disability are not compensable, one would not expect payments to be made within the first week. Table 4-26 basically confirms this, even though there are a few cases reported as being paid within seven days. Over one-third (37 percent) of the compensated cases are paid within the first week after eligibility is established (nearly one-half for the big three). An additional 42 percent are paid within the next two weeks, that is, within the second or third week after eligibility. Less than one claimant in five must wait as long as 30 days for the first benefit check. For the self-insured population, it is only one in ten.

This measure of timeliness could be regarded as somewhat unfair by insurers, since the waiting period is counted as a payment delay in table 4-26, when the insurer may not know that the claim is compensable until the seven days have passed. Table 4-27 shows that there is even less delay when the interval is measured from the first day that was actually compensated until the date of the payment. By this criterion, about 85 percent of unlitigated cases are paid within 30 days.

Analysis by insurer type shows that 80 percent of carrier cases and 92 percent of self-insured cases meet this test of timeliness of payment for unlitigated cases. Presumably the

Table 4-26
Last Day of Work to Date of First Payment by Insurer Type
Unlitigated Cases

Last day of work to date of first payment	Total		Insurer type					
			Carrier		Big three		Other self-insurers	
	Number	Percent	Number	Percent	Number	Percent	Number	Percent
1 to 7 days	20	2.4	8	1.6	3	2.6	9	4.0
8 to 14 days	307	37.0	170	34.8	56	47.9	81	36.2
15 to 30 days	350	42.2	191	39.1	47	40.2	112	50.0
31 to 60 days	112	13.5	84	17.2	8	6.8	20	8.9
61 to 120 days	28	3.4	26	5.3	0	0.0	2	0.9
Over 120 days	13	1.6	10	2.0	3	2.6	0	0.0
Total	830	100.0	489	100.0	117	100.0	224	100.0
			$\bar{X}=28.2$		$\bar{X}=31.9$		$\bar{X}=19.1$	
Missing cases	124							
Grand total	954							

Chi-square = 43.25** with 10 degrees of freedom.
Columns may not add to total due to rounding.

Table 4-27

First Day Compensated to Date of First Payment by Insurer Type
Unlitigated Cases

First day compensated to date of first payment		Insurer type						
	Total		Carrier		Big three		Other self-insurers	
	Number	Percent	Number	Percent	Number	Percent	Number	Percent
0 to 7 days	105	11.9	56	10.5	19	15.8	30	13.0
8 to 14 days	362	41.0	198	37.1	66	55.0	98	42.4
15 to 30 days	282	31.9	171	32.1	26	21.7	85	36.8
31 to 60 days	99	11.2	75	14.1	8	6.7	16	6.9
Over 60 days	36	4.1	33	6.2	1	0.8	2	0.9
Total	884	100.0	533	100.0	120	100.0	231	100.0
Missing cases	70							
Grand total	954							

Chi-square = 40.83** with 8 degrees of freedom.
Columns may not add to total due to rounding.

extra layer of bureaucracy involved in notification to the carrier by the employer accounts for the extra delay in cases from the carrier sector. There is no information in the case records about when the carrier was notified of the injury, so this cannot be investigated with the present data base. There is also no way of determining what the source of delay may be in the slower cases, nothing in the case records suggests any particular cause. In any event, the conclusion is that for unlitigated cases the payment delays are not intolerable. The bulk of the cases are processed and paid without major incident. Unfortunately, litigated cases are another matter entirely.

Litigated

The important dates are not the same for litigated and unlitigated cases, and it will not be possible to reach such a quick judgment on the timeliness question. But the same basic philosophy of dividing the delay into that portion due to recognition or manifestation of the disability and actual payment delay will be followed. In addition, for the litigated cases the administrative delays will be highlighted since this is an area where policy could have a significant impact.

As was pointed out in chapter 3, nearly half of all litigated cases involve claims of multiple injuries; one-quarter show multiple injury dates. Thus the question of when the injury occurred, or exactly what the injury was, is not easy to answer in many litigated cases. For the purposes of analysis, the last injury date reported will be used. This may distort the timeliness measures somewhat, particularly since the Michigan statute defines the last day of work as the injury date for occupational diseases and injuries not attributable to a single event. Relative to the magnitude of litigation delays, however, this will not be a major problem.

Table 4-28 shows the elapsed time from the last injury date to the date of application for hearing by insurer type. For

Table 4-28
Last Injury to Application for Hearing by Insurer Type

Last injury to application for hearing	Total		Insurer type					
			Carrier		Big three		Other self-insurers	
	Number	Percent	Number	Percent	Number	Percent	Number	Percent
To 1 month	118	10.9	53	10.0	48	12.8	17	9.5
1 to 3 months	163	15.0	81	15.3	58	15.4	24	13.4
3 to 6 months	169	15.6	91	17.2	50	13.3	28	15.6
6 to 12 months	174	16.0	95	17.9	50	13.3	29	16.2
1 to 2 years	199	18.3	87	16.4	74	19.7	38	21.2
2 to 4 years	156	14.4	74	14.0	54	14.4	28	15.6
4 to 8 years	78	7.2	36	6.8	29	7.7	13	7.3
Over 8 years	28	2.6	13	2.5	13	3.5	2	1.1
Total	1,085	100.0	530	100.0	376	100.0	179	100.0
Missing cases	139		$\bar{X} = 531$		$\bar{X} = 605$		$\bar{X} = 492$	
Grand total	1,224		(days)		(days)		(days)	

Chi-square = 12.77 with 14 degrees of freedom.
Columns may not add to total due to rounding.

nearly 25 percent of litigated cases, there is a gap of more than two years from the injury date to the initiation of the litigated claim. Over half the litigated cases are initiated within one year of the injury date, but only 11 percent within one month. Of course there is no way of telling directly what was happening in the interim. It is possible that the claimant was trying to establish his or her claim throughout the period and only resorted to the litigation procedure as a last resort. It is safe to assume in other cases that the first the employer or insurer ever hears of the injury is when the application for hearing is served. Whatever the reason, it is astonishing that these litigated cases are already so old at their origin. The average litigated case is already 550 days old when the claim is initiated. It is also worth noting that there is no statistically significant difference among insurer types in this application delay.

Table 4-29 shows that the application delay is less pronounced when measured from the last day of work. Over 30 percent of the litigated cases involve a gap of more than one year from termination of employment to claim initiation. Presumably this reflects claims from retirees and occupational disease and cumulative trauma cases. Clearly, the first important delay in compensation for litigated workers' compensation claims in Michigan arises at the claimant level. The claims for compensation themselves are certainly not timely. On the average, exactly one year has elapsed since the last day of work when a litigated workers' compensation claim enters the system.

Table 4-30 makes it clear that the system also contributes to delays, however. According to the sample cases in the MCCS, only about 26 percent of all litigated cases reach a hearing in less than 12 months from application. More than 15 percent of the litigated cases take over 24 months to come to a hearing. There are significant differences by insurer type

Table 4-29
Last Day of Work to Application for Hearing by Insurer Type

Last day of work to application for hearing	Total		Carrier		Insurer type			
					Big three		Other self-insurers	
	Number	Percent	Number	Percent	Number	Percent	Number	Percent
To 1 month	119	16.2	50	14.6	52	20.1	17	13.0
1 to 3 months	139	19.0	69	20.1	50	19.3	20	15.3
3 to 6 months	121	16.5	58	16.9	37	14.3	26	19.8
6 to 12 months	124	16.9	67	19.5	29	11.2	28	21.4
1 to 2 years	130	17.7	54	15.7	54	20.8	22	16.8
2 to 4 years	65	8.9	33	9.6	24	9.3	8	6.1
4 to 8 years	28	3.8	8	2.3	11	4.2	9	6.9
Over 8 years	7	1.0	4	1.2	2	0.8	1	0.8
Total	733	100.0	343	100.0	259	100.0	131	100.0
Missing cases	491		$\bar{X}=352$		$\bar{X}=355$		$\bar{X}=369$	
Grand total	1,224		(days)		(days)		(days)	

Chi-square = 23.87* with 14 degrees of freedom.
Columns may not add to total due to rounding.

Table 4-30
Application for Hearing to Hearing by Insurer Type

Application for hearing to hearing	Total		Insurer type					
			Carrier		Big three		Other self-insurers	
	Number	Percent	Number	Percent	Number	Percent	Number	Percent
To 6 months	18	2.1	15	3.6	0	0.0	3	2.1
6 to 12 months	204	23.9	127	30.7	52	17.4	25	17.7
12 to 18 months	364	42.7	166	40.1	134	45.0	64	45.4
18 to 24 months	133	15.6	56	13.5	51	17.1	26	18.4
24 to 36 months	89	10.4	34	8.2	43	14.4	12	8.5
Over 36 months	45	5.3	16	3.9	18	6.0	11	7.8
Total	853	100.0	414	100.0	298	100.0	141	100.0
Missing cases	371		$\bar{X} = 493$ (days)		$\bar{X} = 597$ (days)		$\bar{X} = 565$ (days)	
Grand total	1,224							

Chi-square = 40.34** with 10 degrees of freedom.
Columns may not add to total due to rounding.

with the carrier segment showing less delay than the self-insured. Nevertheless, the overwhelming impression is of very considerable delays in adjudication with an average of 540 days from application to hearing date.

These long delays are the consequence of an overburdened adjudicative system, but they also serve to reinforce the duality in Michigan's workers' compensation system. Such delays make it impossible for a disabled worker who requires income maintenance immediately to resort to the system. Thus the original function of the hearings process is frustrated and it is converted even more completely to a lump-sum impairment system inhabited primarily by claimants with another source of income.

In addition, the structure of attorneys' fees in the Michigan system does not reward swiftness. In cases where weekly benefits are awarded, attorneys are allowed up to 30 percent of the accrued liability. The incentives here are too obvious. The interesting question is what would be the delay in reaching a hearing if the large number of cases that do not go to a full hearing of the facts (i.e., redemptions) were not present to clog the adjudication system.

Table 4-31 adds the application delay and the administrative hearing delay together to measure the total time elapsed from the last day of work to the date of the hearing. Recalling the distinction developed earlier between the date of application for hearing and the last injury date, this table provides a measure of the evidentiary problems in adjudicating these claims. Less than 10 percent of litigated claim hearings involve parties who have been in an employer to employee relationship in the last year.

Almost half of the cases involve parties who have not been associated with each other for the last two years. Earlier evidence made clear that this does not reflect a long period of

Table 4-31
Last Day of Work to Hearing by Insurer Type

| Last day of work to hearing | Total | | Insurer type | | | | | | |
| | | | Carrier | | Big three | | Other self-insurers | |
	Number	Percent	Number	Percent	Number	Percent	Number	Percent
To 1 month	1	0.2	1	0.3	0	0.0	0	0.0
6 to 12 months	45	7.0	35	11.7	5	2.2	5	4.2
1 to 2 years	279	43.4	124	41.6	106	46.7	49	41.5
2 to 4 years	222	34.5	97	32.6	81	35.7	44	37.3
4 to 8 years	80	12.4	32	10.7	30	13.2	18	15.3
Over 8 years	16	2.5	9	3.0	5	2.2	2	1.7
Total	643	100.0	298	100.0	227	100.0	118	100.0
			$\bar{X}=912$		$\bar{X}=964$		$\bar{X}=974$	
			(days)		(days)		(days)	
Missing cases	581							
Grand total	1,224							

Chi-square = 23.33** with 10 degrees of freedom.
Columns may not add to total due to rounding.

disability with weekly compensation payments, but rather a severance of the employment relationship for the duration of the delay in most cases. The litigation system is attempting to cope with very old injuries in disputes among employers and employees who probably have trouble remembering each other. For the average litigated case, it is 943 days since the last day of work at the time of the hearing. This is truly an impossible burden.

The last table relating to timeliness of benefits measures the total administrative life of litigated cases from the perspective of the Bureau of Workers' Disability Compensation. Table 4-32 shows the time from the application for hearing to the report of Stopping of Compensation Payments (Form 102), which signals the Bureau that all payments have been completed and the case is ready to be retired. This measure should not be taken to represent a payment delay, since it includes the administrative delays plus any weekly benefit payment duration that results from the litigation process. But it does represent the tracking burden on the Bureau resulting from the litigation rate. Over 80 percent of litigated workers' compensation cases are in the system more than a year, 20 percent for more than two years. This is quite astonishing when it is realized that most of them are simply compromised out anyway. This is a tremendous administrative burden to pay for very little return in terms of actual claims adjudication.

Table 4-32
Application for Hearing to Form 102 by Insurer Type

| Application for hearing to Form 102 | Total | | Insurer type | | | | | |
| | | | Carrier | | Big three | | Other self-insurers | |
	Number	Percent	Number	Percent	Number	Percent	Number	Percent
To 1 month	5	0.6	5	1.2	0	0.0	0	0.0
1 to 3 months	5	0.6	2	0.5	1	0.3	2	1.3
3 to 6 months	16	1.8	11	2.6	4	1.3	1	0.7
6 to 12 months	153	17.3	98	22.7	40	13.2	15	10.1
1 to 2 years	522	59.0	237	55.0	187	61.5	98	65.8
2 to 4 years	143	16.2	62	14.4	57	18.8	24	16.1
4 to 8 years	34	3.8	13	3.0	13	4.3	8	5.4
Over 8 years	6	0.7	3	0.7	2	0.7	1	0.7
Total	884	100.0	431	100.0	304	100.0	149	100.0
Missing cases	340		$\bar{X}=505$		$\bar{X}=619$		$\bar{X}=630$	
Grand total	1,224		(days)		(days)		(days)	

Chi-square = 31.47** with 14 degrees of freedom.
Columns may not add to total due to rounding.

Conclusions to this examination of the timeliness of benefits for litigated cases seem anticlimactic. The application delays are so massive as to make the whole question of delays irrelevant. Obviously the litigation process in Michigan's workers' compensation system bears little resemblance to a no-fault system. As has been suggested earlier, it looks remarkably like a tort liability system. The major difference is that the sums in contention in these proceedings are quite modest.

NOTES

1. There is some overlap with material discussed in chapter 2, where the overview of compensation payments was presented. There will be a good deal more detail presented here, however.

2. *Jolliff v. American Advertising,* 49 Mich App 1. This was recently reversed in *Gussler v. Fairview,* Michigan Supreme Court, No. 63538, December 30, 1981.

3. The Michigan legislature saw fit in 1980 to completely revise the benefit formula. Almost all workers will now receive 80 percent of after-tax pay.

4. See chapter 1 for the discussion of this issue and the comparison of empirical results under the two alternative sampling strategies.

5. See Peter S. Barth with H. Allan Hunt, *Workers' Compensation and Work-Related Illnesses and Diseases* (Cambridge, MA: MIT Press, 1980), for an analysis of the occupational disease problem in workers' compensation.

6. For an earlier study of lump-sum payments in Michigan, see James N. Morgan, Marvin Snider, and Marion G. Sobol, *Lump Sum Redemption Settlements and Rehabilitation: A Study of Workmen's Compensation in Michigan* (Ann Arbor, MI: Institute for Social Research, University of Michigan, 1959).

SUMMARY and CONCLUSIONS   5

This monograph began with the technical description of the data base, the Michigan Closed Case Survey, because that is really what the monograph is about. This volume is *not* a guide to the Michigan workers' compensation system; it makes no pretense of being a complete review of the way workers' compensation functions in Michigan. What the monograph *does* try to do is use one special kind of data source, a closed case survey, to measure the adequacy and timeliness of benefits for Michigan workers disabled by accidents or illnesses arising out of their employment.

The question of sampling design takes on special importance in the context of this descriptive approach. If the data base does not adequately represent the workers' compensation system, a description of the data base is not very valuable. For this reason, extensive attention was given to the various strategies for sampling from a dynamic workers' compensation population in chapter 1. Each sampling strategy was found to have its strengths and weaknesses.

The closed case strategy adopted here tends to produce a picture of the workers' compensation system that under-represents the long disability duration cases. The advantage of the closed case strategy is that it minimizes uncertainty about the outcomes; the sample can be collected at one point in time without waiting for straggler cases to be resolved. The discussion in chapter 1 also made the point that in Michigan there is very little alternative to a closed case design if one must depend on the state's records of the workers' compensation cases. There simply was no other feasible way to sample from the population in the actual situation that presented itself in 1978.

Examination of the completed sample and comparison to other sources of information about the Michigan workers' compensation case population showed that the actual biases of the closed case design were much less than feared. There was an apparent deficit of long duration weekly payment cases, but when durations were imputed for the lump-sum settlements, the Michigan Closed Case Survey (MCCS) actually showed more cases with duration over four years than the insurance industry found using the opposite methodology.

Comparison of the MCCS to official Bureau of Workers' Disability Compensation case statistics for 1978 showed that the sample appropriately represented the insurer population as well. Insurance carriers and self-insurers were represented in correct proportions and the large individual insurers also seemed to be represented in the appropriate numbers in the data base. There was one problem revealed by the comparison to Bureau statistics, though. The MCCS does not contain enough judges' opinions or cases withdrawn before adjudication or dismissed by the judge.

This apparently reflected an unexpected seasonality problem. While these cases were retired by the Bureau in October and November of 1978, the decisions had come primarily from the month of August. It is assumed that the problems with the sample reflect the incidence of summer vacations for the administrative law judges. Nevertheless, the conclusion was that, overall, the MCCS provided an adequate empirical representation of Michigan's workers' compensation case population in 1978.

Chapter 2 presented an empirical overview of the Michigan workers' compensation experience.[1] It employed a weighted combination of the litigated and unlitigated samples to report statistics on claimant characteristics, the origin of the claim, and the amount and duration of compensation. The primary conclusion from this examination was that commercial workers' compensation insurance carriers and self-insured employers are quite different in almost every dimension of workers' compensation experience.

This result highlights the major contribution of the MCCS, the ability to compare different insurer types. To take maximum advantage of this fact, most analyses have been organized by type of insurer. Throughout the monograph, the fact repeatedly emerges that carriers and self-insurers demonstrate very different workers' compensation experiences. This is most striking for the big three auto producers. In the proportion of cases litigated, for instance, the big three experience a 48 percent litigation rate while carriers only show 22 percent and self-insurers other than the big three 19 percent. These differences are very highly significant statistically.

Chapter 2 also demonstrates that despite the degree of contention, the voluntary payment cases are still dominant. Nearly three-fourths of Michigan workers' compensation claims are voluntarily paid by the insurers. Nevertheless, major attention is directed to the issue of litigation in this monograph. There are three reasons for this. First is the question of the role of litigation in a workers' compensation system designed 70 years ago to eliminate litigation. It was dissatisfaction with the litigious approach to compensating injured workers early in this century that led to the no-fault principle upon which workers' compensation programs were built.

Second, in a theoretical context, the wage-loss principle and lump-sum settlements are generally regarded as mutually exclusive. Yet in Michigan these are two of the main characteristics of the workers' compensation system. This calls for some explanation. Last, a major share of the Bureau of Workers' Disability Compensation administrative burden arises from the litigated case population. For this reason alone, the extent of litigation and the function of litigation in the workers' compensation system in Michigan are worthy of study.

Analysis in chapter 2 shows that the method of resolution, geographical location, nature of injury, part of body injured, level of disability, reason payments ended, gender and age of claimant, number of dependents, weekly earnings, and the weekly benefit amount all differ significantly by insurer type. These results represent the working of a number of influences, including the wage levels, the worker population covered, and the extent of litigation among the different insurer groups.

The extent of litigation plays a strong explanatory role because litigated cases are so different from unlitigated cases. In general, the data available in the MCCS come from different sources for litigated and unlitigated cases. In both samples the collection of the data was oriented to the administrative reports to the Bureau of Workers' Disability Compensation. Since most of the information about litigated cases originates in the process of litigation itself, it is very strongly tainted by the process.

This may be best illustrated in the seemingly simple descriptions of the nature of the injury claimed and the part of the body affected. For unlitigated cases these data come from a report filed by the employer at the time of the injury. For litigated cases, they come from the Petition for Hearing, which is the form that originates a litigated case. Inasmuch as this document establishes the scope of the claim (and eventually the scope of the settlement) and since it is usually written by the claimant's attorney, the description of the nature of the injury and the part of the body affected take on a rather special mission. This culminates in the claim for what has come to be called by some critics of the system "an injury to the skin and its contents." The boiler-plate approach to describing the source of a worker's claimed disability makes it very difficult to determine from the official case documents just what the injury really was.

From the point of the statistical tests of significant differences among insurer types in chapter 2, the approach also produces a possibly spurious result. Since the proportion of litigated cases differs by insurer type, the stylized litigation process itself strongly affects the comparisons. Because of the boiler-plate approach to the claimed injuries in litigated cases, they are frequently coded as multiple injuries. But if the incidence of litigated cases is much higher for the big three, the incidence of multiple injuries is also much higher. This leads to the conclusion that the proportion of different types of injuries varies systematically with insurer type. What cannot be determined is whether there is more litigation because there are more multiple injuries, or whether there are more multiple injuries reported because there is more litigation.

The incidence of litigation and the consequent incidence of lump-sum settlements (called redemptions in Michigan) combined with the wage-loss philosophy of the Michigan statute produce another problem in describing workers' compensation in Michigan. It is not possible to divide Michigan cases into the traditional disability categories of fatality, permanent total, permanent partial, temporary total and medical only. Since the disability category cannot be determined in a lump-sum case, the results in chapter 2 showed that over 20 percent of all cases could not be allocated. In addition, since the Bureau of Workers' Disability Compensation in Michigan does not require reporting on medical expenses for individual cases, there are no medical only cases included in the data base.

The review of the actual compensation paid to the claimants represented in the MCCS revealed a number of interesting facts. First and foremost, the restricted scope of the statutory two-thirds income replacement rate was shown. In 1978 only 20 percent of weekly payment cases actually received a benefit that equaled two-thirds of their earnings. This result reflects a complex interaction between Michigan's maximum benefit, the dependency allowance, and the minimum benefit.[2]

The maximum weekly benefit in Michigan is set at two-thirds the previous year's state average weekly wage. But to receive that amount, a disabled worker must have both a weekly earnings level at or above the state average and the maximum of five or more dependents. With fewer dependents, the maximum benefit is reduced. Thus a disabled worker with no dependents would only be eligible for a maximum benefit that represents 55 percent of the state average weekly wage. If such a worker happened to earn exactly the state average wage, he or she could not attain the two-thirds replacement rate specified in the statute because of the maximum benefit limitation. In essence, the maximum benefit is reduced to less than two-thirds the state average weekly wage for most injured workers. As a result, nearly 64 percent of the weekly payment cases receive the maximum weekly compensation rate for their dependency classification.

On the other hand, Michigan has very high minimum benefits. This results from an appeals court decision tying the minimum benefit to the same absolute annual dollar adjustment as provided by statute for the maximum benefits.[3]

The effect of this adjustment has been to narrow the relative gap between minimum and maximum benefit levels very significantly over the years. It is shown in chapter 4 that for a disabled worker with three dependents the 1968 minimum was 44 percent of the maximum benefit level. But by 1978 the minimum had risen to 72 percent of the maximum. In 1978 some 15 percent of all weekly benefit cases received the minimum benefit, as did over 20 percent of the cases closed by insurance carriers.

It was demonstrated in chapter 4 that this benefit structure provides widely varying income replacement proportions. About 15 percent of unlitigated workers' compensation cases in Michigan receive less than 40 percent gross wage replacement. On the other end of the scale, 3 percent achieve over 100 percent and another 10 percent get from 70 to 100 percent replacement of their weekly gross earnings. The most logical conclusion is simply that the benefit structure got out of adjustment over the years since 1969 with no legislative attention.[4]

Turning to the duration of weekly benefit payments, it was seen that here the experience did not differ by insurer type. Weekly payment cases closed by carriers and self-insurers showed similar duration distributions. This was true for both litigated and unlitigated cases and represents one of the few areas of the study where no significant differences among insurer types could be found.

It is well-known that most workers' compensation cases are of rather short duration. The MCCS demonstrates that half the weekly payment cases in Michigan have durations of less than four weeks. Less than 10 percent show durations over 26 weeks, although this result is affected by the closed case sampling bias and should be treated more carefully. In chapter 4 an attempt was made to determine the impact of the waiting week reimbursement provision of Michigan law.

Since the first, or waiting, week is only compensated if the disability lasts two weeks or more, one might expect claimants would be increasingly loath to return to work as they near the end of their second week of disability. If there is such an effect, it is not obvious in the disability distribution examined here. The conclusion is that the malingering claimed by some cannot be demonstrated to be a major problem.

The product of the weekly compensation rate and the duration of weekly benefits is of course the total weekly compensation paid. The results of the analysis of total weekly compensation paid by insurer type were very interesting. While the durations of payment did not differ significantly by insurer, the weekly compensation rates did, so the total weekly payments were expected to show significant differences as well.

In fact, there was a statistically significant difference in total weekly compensation when all cases were considered in chapter 2. But this resulted from the differences in the proportions of litigated cases for different insurer types. Since those litigated cases that received weekly payments got about seven times as much on the average as unlitigated cases, the differing proportion of litigated cases produced significant differences when all cases were considered together. In chapter 2 it was shown that the big three pay 26 percent more and other self-insurers 10 percent less than carriers in weekly compensation to the average case.

But the analysis in chapter 4, which separated litigated and unlitigated cases, did not disclose statistically significant differences between the insurer types. The big three were shown in chapter 4 to pay 18 percent more than carriers in total weekly compensation to the average unlitigated case and 35 percent more to the average litigated case. Other self-insurers pay about 6 percent more to unlitigated and 7 percent less to litigated cases than do carriers. However, these differences were not statistically significant when considered separately for the litigated and unlitigated populations.

As mentioned earlier, there were also a large number of cases in the MCCS that never received any weekly compensation payments at all. In fact, it was shown in chapter 2 that over 20 percent of all Michigan closed cases fell into this category. This group consisted of 7 percent washouts (never received any indemnity payments), and 15 percent that had received lump-sum payments only. Reflecting the litigation experience, there were very striking differences in these proportions by insurer. Nearly one-third of all the big three cases received lump-sum payments only, while this was true for only 11 percent of carrier and other self-insurer cases.

Virtually all of these lump-sum payments are the result of litigation; only a handful represent payments for scheduled losses or advances on future weekly benefits. In the aggregate workers' compensation picture in Michigan, lump-sum payments loom very large. The MCCS indicates that *60 percent* of all the compensation paid over the lifetime of these closed cases was paid in lump-sums rather than weekly payments. This proportion varies by insurer type from 53.6 percent for self-insurers other than the big three to 66.8 percent for the big three auto producers; carriers fall in between at 60.7 percent. Thus all insurer types pay out more dollars in lump-sum payments than in periodic payments, according to the evidence presented here.[5]

It was shown in chapter 4 that the average size of the lump-sum payment also varies widely among insurer types. The average gross lump-sum payment ranged from a high of $10,529 for carriers, to $8,493 for other self-insurers, to $5,659 for the big three. These differences were highly significant statistically. The unique thing about the big three lump-sum distribution is that it has much lower variance than the others. This is hypothesized to be the result of the "routine redemption" in the auto industry.

Many of these routine redemptions involve retired claimants. While it was not possible to identify the retirement status of all claimants, it was estimated in chapter 3 that from 25 to 35 percent cf all litigated cases were filed by retirees. Estimates by insurer type were 15 to 20 percent for carriers, 30 to 40 percent for other self-insurers, and 40 to 50 percent for the big three. Further, these retired claimants received a minimum of 18 percent of all the indemnity payments reported in the MCCS. This proportion ranged from 10 percent for carrier claims, to 20 percent for other self-insurers, and an incredible 40 percent for the big three.

When attention is turned from the cost of lump-sum payments (gross amount) to the lump-sum benefit actually received by the claimant (net amount), there are a number of adjustments required. Clearly, the costs of litigation must be deducted since they are not received as benefits by the claimant. The MCCS showed that these costs run between 20 and 25 percent of the gross lump-sum. This covers the attorney's fee, medical examination and deposition, and other legal expenses.

In addition, 18 percent of all lump-sum payment cases show a designated amount "reserved for future medical care." It is paid to the claimant at the time of settlement but is supposed to be used to pay for future medical costs arising from the disability. This apparently is an adaptation to avoid the objections some have to compromise and release settlements when future medical costs are no longer provided for. For those lump-sum cases showing such medical cost designations, the average amount is 57 percent of the gross lump-sum. These payments are excluded from the net lump-sum figure in the analysis here on the grounds that no other medical costs are included, so these should not be counted as benefit payments either.[6]

The average gross lump-sum payment to the cases in the MCCS was $8,551. After deducting the litigation expenses and the funds reserved for future medical costs, the average lump-sum received by the claimant (net lump-sum) was $5,944. As with the gross lump-sum amounts, there were significant differences by insurer type. The average lump-sum received by a big three claimant was $3,777, while other self-insurer's claimants realized $6,186 and carrier's claimants, $7,336.

When a multivariate regression analysis was done on the net lump-sum payments, it was found that the size of the net lump-sum varied directly with the previous earnings level and the amount paid earlier in weekly compensation. Self-insurers were shown by this regression to pay significantly smaller lump-sums than carriers. There was also a positive relationship between the size of the lump-sum and previous repeated spells of disability, a record of hospitalization, or a claim of a back injury. It is hypothesized that a previous demonstrable disability lends some credence to a litigated claim. Thus earlier weekly payments or hospitalization tend to indicate legitimacy of the claim and hence are correlated with higher lump-sum payments. Unfortunately, the data were not detailed enough to warrant additional analysis, so these conclusions must be regarded as somewhat tentative.

In profiling average total compensation payments by insurer type, some interesting patterns emerge. In comparison to insurance carriers, the big three pay more than twice as many lump-sum cases, but they pay only about half as much to each. The big three pay relatively fewer weekly compensation cases, but they pay a higher weekly rate. When all is said and done, the average indemnity received by each carrier claimant in the MCCS was $2,319. For big three claimants it was $2,303.

Self-insurers other than the big three paid a similar proportion of weekly cases to that of carriers, but they paid them a slightly higher weekly rate for a slightly shorter period of time. In lump-sum payment cases, they paid fewer dollars on the average to relatively fewer cases. Thus the average total indemnity received by other self-insurers' claimants was $1,921, or about 17 percent less than that for carriers or the big three.

When all indemnity payments are measured in terms of disability duration, through imputing durations to lump-sum cases by dividing the net lump-sum payments by the mean weekly compensation rate for the corresponding insurer type, much the same result is found. The average successful workers' compensation claim against insurance carriers receives 23.6 weeks worth of benefits. The average big three claimant receives 23.7 weeks. The average claim against self-insurers other than the big three receives 16.9 weeks worth of benefits, nearly 30 percent less.

This advantage derives primarily from the litigated case experience. Self-insurers other than the big three actually demonstrate slightly higher average compensation totals than carriers for unlitigated cases. But they have both a lower incidence of litigation and a lower average cost for litigated cases when compared to carriers. Unfortunately, the MCCS does not contain sufficient detail to carry this comparative analysis any further, but the differences are certainly large enough to give these self-insurers a considerable advantage in workers' compensation costs.

When the issue of the timeliness of benefit payments was addressed in chapter 4, it was shown that in 80 to 85 percent of unlitigated cases in Michigan, the claimant receives a benefit check within 30 days. Depending on the specific measurement used, from 40 to 50 percent have checks within 14 days. No matter how timeliness is measured, the big three do the best job, followed by other self-insurers, and the carriers coming in consistently last. As an example, when the measurement is from the last day of work to the date of initial payment, in 50 percent of their cases the big three get a check out within 14 days. The corresponding figures are 40 percent and 36 percent for other self-insurers and carriers, respectively.

Turning to litigated cases, the question of timeliness really loses its meaning in Michigan's workers' compensation system. The delays are so massive, it is obvious that timeliness is not regarded as an important criterion by those involved in the system—beginning with the claimant. It was shown in chapter 4 that the average time elapsed from the date of last injury to the application for hearing is over 500 days. Almost 25 percent of litigated claims are filed more than two years after the injury; almost 10 percent are not filed until more than four years following the injury.

It is unlikely that this reflects the incidence of long latency occupational diseases, since in such cases Michigan law dictates that the last day of work shall be designated as the day of injury. Yet when the application delay is measured from the last day of work, the average delay remains over 350 days. Presumably the long application delays reflect a combination of circumstances.

Some occupational diseases and cumulative trauma conditions do take substantial periods of time to manifest themselves. In addition, in the presence of such potentially disabling conditions, workers frequently have some option as to when they choose to file. As long as one can continue to do the work, perhaps it is better to wait until there really is no alternative before going through the hassle of a workers' compensation claim. This is particularly clear if the worker expects to encounter resistance from the employer, and anticipates that once the claim has been filed, there is little chance of going back to work. Under these circumstances, it might be possible that a worker could delay filing the claim for some time, possibly even until a separation occurs for other reasons.

On the other hand, it may be (as many employers believe) that workers encounter a workers' compensation plaintiff attorney somehow and become bewitched with the prospect of easy money. This may also be more likely if the employment relationship is already severed. The attorney takes the case on a contingency fee, and all the claimant has to do is submit to two physical exams and possibly a few hours at a hearing some time in the future. Under this scenario, the statute of limitations does not provide an effective bar to claims because in Michigan the time under the statute of limitations does not begin to toll until the employer has notified the Bureau of the injury. Obviously, if the employer is not aware of the injury, the statute of limitations does not come into play. Both of these scenarios are consistent with litigated claims that are old when they are filed. No doubt there are others as well.

The timeliness results presented in chapter 4 for litigated cases made it clear that the administration by the Bureau of Workers' Disability Compensation contributes to the delays as well. The average time elapsed between the application for hearing and the actual hearing itself for the cases in the MCCS was also well over 500 days. Only about 25 percent of litigated cases come to a hearing within one year of initiation of the claim. Then, after all this delay, fully 70 percent of these cases are redeemed with a compromise and release settlement that involves only a *pro-forma* approval of the agreement. Whether the hearings process contributed to this resolution in any substantial way is not clear. It is obvious that the whole process is enormously inefficient by the standards of a no-fault insurance system.

Chapter 3 contained a rather extensive analysis of the correlates of litigation. While it was disappointing overall due to the lack of information on litigated cases that was not tainted by the litigation process, a number of interesting results were obtained. First, as mentioned earlier, multiple injuries and multiple parts of the body were very strongly correlated with litigation. This reflects the boiler-plate approach to injury allegations on the application for hearing. There was also a high correlation of litigation with impairment of entire body systems, i.e., respiratory, circulatory, etc.

Since the Petition for Hearing contains a separate line item for occupational disease claims, some have alleged that this encourages adding any potential occupational disease to a litigated claim no matter what the claim is really about. But in 26 percent of the litigated cases, only occupational disease is claimed. The different insurer types show very significant differences in this regard also, with the proportion of straight occupational disease claims ranging from 19 percent for carriers to 23 percent for other self-insurers and 37 percent for the big three.

This examination stops well short of alleging that the litigation problem in Michigan's workers' compensation system is strictly an occupational disease problem, however. This is due both to the data problems discussed earlier, and to the judgment that the occupational disease problem is not of sufficient magnitude to account for the amount of litigation present in the Michigan system.

The analysis in chapter 3 also showed that back injuries were significantly more likely to be litigated, while simple injuries like burns, cuts, and fractures were significantly less

likely than other injuries to become enmeshed in the litigation process. It was also shown that fatality claims were
much more likely to be litigated. These factors taken
together are indicative of the evidentiary problems that
plague the workers' compensation system. The facts are
quite clear in a fracture case; the accident happened and it is
either compensable or not, depending primarily on where
and when it happened. Even though workers' compensation
is a no-fault system, there is little chance that an employee
would claim benefits for a fracture that occurred at home.
The system only protects workers' incomes against injuries
and diseases arising out of and in the course of employment.

Occupational diseases, cumulative trauma injuries, and
some fatalities can present a different aspect, however. The
specific etiology of the disabling condition can be quite
obscure.[7] In addition, a liberal interpretation of the workers'
compensation statute (particularly through the contributory
factor or acceleration of the disease process areas of the
definition of disability) would make it possible to bring nearly all the ordinary diseases of life suffered by employees into
the system. So the employers react by contesting what they
regard as dubious claims. One is then presented with the
anomaly of a no-fault system devoting a great deal of time to
fighting over what is covered and what is not. The old tort
liability disputes over *who* is at fault are simply replaced by
disputes over *what* is at fault.

Another important influence on the likelihood of litigation developed in chapter 3 is insurer type. Results there
showed that cases from the big three are significantly more
likely and cases from other self-insurers significantly less
likely to be litigated than are insurance carrier cases. This
phenomenon has been discussed repeatedly through the
monograph. It should be noted that this result comes from a
multivariate analysis; thus it represents the correlation of insurer type with litigation holding constant other factors such

as type of injury, age and sex of the claimant, indemnity level and location.

The MCCS cannot prove what caused the litigation, but merely notes its presence as a demonstrable fact. In this instance, it cannot be shown conclusively whether the big three are more likely to contest a claim of given "worthiness," or whether the employees of the big three are inclined to file claims that are less "worthy" on the average than other employees. On the other hand, self-insurers other than the big three experience less litigation. It is tempting to say that they are doing a better job of claims management (in the large sense, i.e., including preventing claims from reaching the litigious state), but the MCCS cannot prove this either. It will therefore have to be sufficient to conclude that the big three experience more litigation and other self-insurers less litigation than the carrier sector. This issue clearly warrants further study.

There are two more case characteristics that demonstrated association with litigation in chapter 3. Cases from Detroit and cases involving claimants age 55 or over were shown to be significantly more likely to be litigated than others. The impact of the large industrial urban center on the tendency to litigate is well-known; this turns up in most analyses of income maintenance systems. Things are done differently in Miami, Los Angeles, Chicago, Detroit or New York than in smaller places. There is what Monroe Berkowitz twenty years ago dubbed a greater "claims consciousness" in highly industrialized urban environments.[8] Whether due to more attorneys, stronger unions, better information networks, or some kind of socio-psychological differences, it is not a surprise that it turns up in the Michigan workers' compensation system as well.

The higher tendency to litigation among older workers is not a surprise either. Nearly everyone has heard about the "retiree problem" in Michigan's workers' compensation system. According to results presented earlier, between one-fourth and one-third of all litigated cases are filed by retirees; these cases receive nearly 20 percent of all indemnity payments in Michigan.

The magnitude of retiree claims in the litigated case population seems to make a mockery of the wage-loss principle of indemnity, supposedly the philosophical foundation of the Michigan workers' compensation law. This is not to say these claimants are undeserving, but by definition a worker who is *voluntarily* retired from the workforce cannot be suffering wage loss as a result of a disability. The "opportunity" to suffer a wage loss has been foregone in the election of retirement.

Redemptions are popular with most, if not all, participants in the system. The claimants appreciate getting the money in a lump-sum, even if it takes two to three years to get it. The claimant's attorney prefers it since the fee comes off the top of the settlement and collection costs for professional services are minimized. The insurers seem to like redemptions because they eliminate uncertainty by cashing out disability claims with a fixed dollar figure and by prohibiting future claims from the same source. Finally, the Bureau of Workers' Disability Compensation seems to like redemption settlements because they minimize the administrative burden of the litigation system.

The major requirement for securing a redemption settlement in Michigan is probably the source of income to make it possible to wait out the long delay until the case is settled. This is one of the reasons so many retiree claims are flooding the system. Retirees have the time and usually the income support to make a try at a workers' compensation settlement possible. In addition, they can be expected to show some physical impairment after a lifetime of work in the industrial world; plus they are often no longer in need of maintaining the goodwill of their employer.

This is not to question whether a lifetime of work and exposure to industrial hazards is not worth a bonus of a few thousand dollars. It is to ask whether that is the function of the workers' compensation system. It also raises the issue of the impact on an administrative system that does not have the resources to cope with its other responsibilities. Michigan's litigation system is littered with too many dubious claims waiting in line for their redemption settlement. Because of this, more legitimate dispute settlement functions are frustrated. How could an injured worker who needed a weekly paycheck wait through the delays described here? In addition, scarce resources are drained from rehabilitation and other more productive functions to handle the paper deluge. Both the workers' compensation system and the administration of it end up with a serious misallocation of resources.

This study has illuminated, perhaps only dimly, two separate workers' compensation systems in Michigan. The unlitigated system operates much as the theory of workers' compensation would suggest. It is not perfect, of course. It does not provide sufficient support for reemployment efforts. It can be somewhat slow in generating income replacement benefits in some cases. It clearly provides an inadequate level of income replacement for a great many workers. But it looks like a workers' compensation system.

The litigated system resembles a miniature tort liability system; miniature in that the dollar amounts at stake are tiny fractions of those represented in individual tort liability injury claims these days; miniature in that the quality and quantity of proofs required bear only a distant relation to those in a real tort liability action; but full-size in the litigiousness and interminable delays characterizing the process. After 70 years of workers' compensation in Michigan, it is time once again to get tort liability out of the workplace. It is time to turn again to a no-fault wage-loss system of workers' compensation, with administrative procedures designed to meet the needs of the victims of industrial accident and disease; swift medical care, adequate income maintenance, rehabilitation and retraining where required, and most of all, an early return to the ranks of productive society for those workers unfortunate enough to have been disabled by their work.

As mentioned in the first chapter of this monograph, substantial changes have been made in Michigan's workers' compensation system since the data reported here were collected. Many of the flaws discussed have been addressed but the full impact of the changes has yet to be felt. The function of this publication is to provide a standard against which the new system can be measured. Hopefully, when the next study of the Michigan system is undertaken, all these problems will have been resolved.

NOTES

1. There have only been a few published works dealing with the Michigan system. See James N. Morgan, Marvin Snider, and Marion G. Sobol, *Lump Sum Redemption Settlements and Rehabilitation: A Study of Workmen's Compensation in Michigan* (Ann Arbor, MI: Institute for Social Research, University of Michigan, 1959) for an early description of the redemption system in Michigan. Another early study dealing with the cost issue is John F. Burton, Jr., *Interstate Variations in Employers' Costs of Workmen's Compensation: Effect on Plant Location Exemplified in Michigan* (Kalamazoo, MI: W. E. Upjohn Institute for Employment Research, 1966). See also the report of the Governor's Workmen's Compensation Advisory Commission, *Workers' Compensation in Michigan* (Ann Arbor, MI: The Commission, 1975).

2. These issues are discussed more fully in chapter 4.

3. *Jolliff v. American Advertising,* 49 Mich App 1.

4. This is confirmed by the fact that the 1980 reforms totally scrapped the old benefit structure.

5. This conclusion may be subject to qualification due to the closed case bias, since it was pointed out earlier that long duration weekly payment cases will have lower weekly compensation amounts (reflecting wage levels in the past). The downward cost bias for weekly payments introduced by this factor may or may not be matched in the lump-sum payments; there is not enough information available from the litigated cases to tell. So it may not be strictly correct to say that all insurer types pay out more dollars in lump-sums than in periodic payments. The point, however, is that lump-sum payments are very significant in Michigan's workers' compensation system, and any analysis that ignores them starts out with a fatal omission.

6. This procedure was followed even though some have asserted that the "reserved for future medical" category is used simply as a device to avoid social security offset of lump-sum payments.

7. See Barth with Hunt, chapter 3.

8. This is discussed in *Workmen's Compensation: The New Jersey Experience* (New Brunswick: Rutgers University Press, 1960), pp. 26-36.

APPENDIX

Michigan Closed Case Survey

Instructions - Unlitigated Case Sample

I. General Comments
    A. Coverage

        It is intended that all potentially compensable cases should be
        included in the sample whether actually compensated or not.
        There are some cases for which the employer filed Form 100
        even though no lost time (or insufficient lost time) occurred.
        In such cases there is no liability for wage replacement
        benefits and the case should not be included in the sample.
        Aside from these "mistakes" however, all cases are to be
        abstracted.

    B. Organization of Instrument

        The data gathering instrument for the unlitigated case sample
        is strongly oriented to Bureau of Workers' Disability Com-
        pensation Forms 100, 101, and 102. Page one generally cor-
        responds to Form 100 and seeks to identify the injured party,
        the injury, the employer and insurer. Page two will contain
        the information about actual compensation paid while page
        three probes the termination of the case. Thus the organiza-
        tion is chronological and is designed to follow file organiza-
        tion as closely as possible. In Part II below, specific com-
        ments about individual items will be presented.

    C. Missing Data

        The instrument we are using is oriented to Bureau forms in
        the interest of easing the abstracting and coding process.
        However, the questions ultimately are about the cases, not the
        forms. As you know there are frequently items missing from
        these forms. In circumstances where they have an important
        bearing on the case, Bureau personnel will generally have
        followed up to ascertain the facts. In these instances you
        should record the correct information as determined by the
        Bureau.

        In other cases a determination may be possible utilizing infor-
        mation recorded elsewhere in the file. But please note that it is

not a tragedy to have a missing item for a particular case. You are encouraged to use your judgment in walking this fine line. If you are reasonably confident that you know the facts, record them as you understand them. If you are not, leave the item blank and we will take it to be missing.

D. General Format Instructions
   1. Dates

   All dates are to be entered in month-day-year format in the three pairs of boxes allowed. For instance, January 17, 1978 would be recorded as 01-17-78.

   2. Dollar Amounts

   Except in the case of the hourly wage rate, all dollar amounts are to be rounded to the nearest dollar. Amounts of less than 50^c should be dropped while amounts of 50^c or more will be raised to the next higher integer. Thus $176.31 would be 176 while $38.90 would be 39.

   3. Duration

   Compensation duration is to be expressed in weeks and days as on Form 102. Where it is necessary to add two or more separate durations for total compensation duration (all periods), you should follow Bureau practice of assuming a six-day work week. Thus compensation durations of 10 weeks, 4 days and 3 weeks, 3 days should be recorded as a total of 14 weeks, 1 day.

   4. Indented Sections

   Indented sections are those that are contingent upon the answer to the preceeding question. For example, the date of death on page 1 is only relevant if the case was a fatality. These items are to be skipped where not relevant, simply drop down to the next non-indented item.

E. Case Order

It is vital that completed forms be kept in numerical order according to case identification number. This will make it possible to check back to source later if anomalies develop.

II. Comments on Specific Items

Page 1

1. Case identification #
    This is the number stamped on the back of the green sheet at retirement.

*   Name of injured employee
    As entered on Forms 100 and 101, last name first.

25. Date of injury
    If there should be multiple dates of injury that pertain to the same compensable disability, record the earliest.

31. Last day worked
    Where the injured employee may have returned to work subsequent to first disability period, record the last day worked before original disability.

37. Fatality
    If injured employee should die after Form 100 is filed it is still a fatality case. Is Form 106 present?

44. Place of injury
    Code county of injury from item 9 on Form 100.

46. Hospitalization
    If name and address of hospital entered for item 12, Form 100, answer is yes; if not, answer is no. For old format Form 100, answer unknown.

47. Nature of injury
    Follow directions in codebook.

50. Part of body
    Follow directions in codebook.

53. Hours regularly worked per week
    From Form 100, item 16.

55. Straight time hourly wage rate
    Either from Form 100, item 16, or from Form 101, item 7. Do not calculate from weekly earnings unless it is clear that these do not include overtime or other special items.

59. Combined average weekly earnings
    From Form 100. This is to be based on the payroll record calculation. The earnings specifically used for calculating the compensation rate will be collected from Form 101.

62. Self insured number
From Form 100 or code from insurer list in codebook. It is necessary to add 0 where blank, dash, or letter appears in the Bureau's self insurer code number. Code all 8's if self insured and no code number can be located.

70. Insurance Company number
From Form 100 or code from insurer list in codebook. Note State Accident Fund is number 999. Code 888 if carrier given but code number cannot be found.

Page 2

1. Date disability commenced
From Form 101, item 5.

7. Combined weekly earnings (for compensation rate)
Record the earnings actually used to determine the compensation rate from Form 101. In some cases this will be the same as combined average weekly earnings recorded above. In other cases it will be 40 times the hourly wage rate.

10. Number of dependents
Form 101, item 8, or as determined by the Bureau.

11. Date first payment made
As reported on initial Form 101.

17. Date of initial Form 101
This and the items following it refer to the first period of disability following the injury.

23. Initial weekly compensation rate
Weekly rate paid for *first* period of disability following injury. Rounded to nearest dollar.

26. Beginning date for compensation
Record the "From" date on Form 102 for the first period of compensation following injury.

32. End date for compensation
Record the "To" date on Form 102 for the first period of compensation following injury.

38. Compensation duration
From Form 102, in weeks and days, for the first period of compensation following injury.

42. Kind of disability
    Classification of the first period of disability.

43. Number of separate compensation periods
    As indicated on Forms 101 and 102. Separate periods to be differentiated either by a return to work or a change in compensation rate (other than for dependency change).

44. Final weekly compensation rate
    This and the next 4 items all refer to the *last* period of compensation following injury.

47. Beginning date for compensation
    Record the "From" date on Form 102 for the last period of compensation before retirement of case.

53. End date for compensation
    Record the "To" date on Form 102 for the last period of compensation before retirement of case.

59. Compensation duration
    From Form 102, in weeks and days, for the last period of compensation before retirement of case.

63. Kind of disability
    Classification of the last period of disability.

64. Total compensation duration (all periods)
    Sum of durations of separate compensation periods; not calendar elapsed time.

68. Total weekly compensation paid (all periods)
    Sum of dollars paid in weekly benefits over all periods of disability reported for case.

Page 3

1. Reason payments stopped
    As indicated on final Form 102 or from other documents present in file. Dispute refers specifically to insurer filing Form 107 (Notice of dispute). Physician's report refers to those cases where same is not accompanied by Form 107. Benefits expired refers to specific loss or fatality cases, or others where a definite term of weekly benefits was specified.

2. Date of final return to work
   As indicated on final Form 102. If no return to work is indicated, leave this blank.

8. Date of final Form 102
   Date on last Form 102 filed before retirement of case.

14. Form 107 filed?
    Was a Notice of Dispute filed at any time during the life of the case?

15. Date of Form 107
    If more than one, record the date of the last 107.

21. Reason for dispute
    The options are designed as a hierarchy here.

    1. Injury or disability denied means that the insurer denies the existence of any disability.
    2. Work relatedness of disability denied means that while the insurer does not dispute the existence of disability, he denies it arose out of and in the course of employment.
    3. Liability of insurer denied covers situations where the insurer does not deny the disability or its work related origins, but specifically denies his liability. This could be due to lack of notice, multiple employer liability, jurisdiction problems, etc.
    4. Continued disability disputed refers to situations where benefits have been paid but insurer now asserts that individual has recovered.
    5. Degree of impairment disputed refers to situations where insurer claims that injured party is being overcompensated for present degree of disability. Insurer seeks reduction from total to partial disability rating.

22. Mediation applied?
    Was a Compensation Consultant involved in the resolution of the dispute?

23. Outcome of mediation
    Were payments ultimately continued as a result of the mediation effort?

24. Case referred for vocational rehabilitation?
    Letter of referral for VR in the file?

25. Vocational rehabilitation program instituted?
    Is there any record on 110s of any VR program being established for this individual?

26. Encoder
    To identify the individual abstracting the information from case files. To be assigned.

Specific Items - Litigated Case Sample

Page 1

1. Case identification number
   Drop the leading zeroes and record the last 7 digits. Where case has been retired before, take the latest case number.

17. County
    County stamped at upper right hand corner of summary sheet inside folder.

19. Self insured number
    Check final 102 for coding of insurer. Generally not coded for self insurers. Look up employer in coding book and record number. Substitute zero for dashes, blanks, letters or other non-numeric characters.

27. Insurance company number
    Generally coded on final 102. Otherwide proceed as above.

    * If multiple insurer liability
      This is meant to cover the situation where one employer is insured by two or more different carriers over the course of a disablement as well as the situation where two or more employers are involved. If more than 2 insurers, record those against whom the largest compensation liability is eventually assessed.

41. Total number of employers involved
    Simply count number of *employers* listed on summary sheet.

42. Date of AFH
    As listed on summary sheet, date application for hearing received by Bureau.

48. Served and Set
    As recorded on summary sheet.

54. Pre-Trial Conference Date
   As recorded on summary sheet.

60. Claimant Birthdate
   Generally these items identifying the characteristics of the claimant will come from the 104. Do not hesitate to use other sources if it seems advisable.

68. Weekly earnings at time of disablement
   Generally from 104. If not available use other sources. Preferred to daily wage measure on 104.

71. Daily wage at time of disablement
   Alternative to weekly earnings on 104 if they are not reported.

Page 2

1. Last day worked
   Sometimes listed on 104; sometimes noted on summary sheet (if taken as date of injury); sometimes mentioned in medical reports. If no Form 100 this may be difficult. The intent is to gather the last day worked before disablement.

7. Date of injury or disablement
   According to Form 104. Space is available for three separate personal injuries or occupational diseases. These will rarely be easy to choose or code since the tendency is to claim everything that might be work-related. Use your judgment in choosing those that are of major significance. There is no way of telling precisely which injury ends up being compensated. Some guidance is available in medical reports for some cases.

13. Type
   According to whether it is listed as a personal injury or occupational disease on Form 104.

46. Form 100 filed on any of these injuries?
   This is to check for overlap with Form 104 which will generally produce the injuries listed above.

47. Date of Form 100
   Date on the form itself. Take the earliest Form 100 if these were multiples.

53. Fatality?
   Listed on 104 or 100. Check for Form 106.

60. Hospitalization?
    From Form 100, or medical reports. May be difficult.

Page 3
1. Form 107 filed?
   Was a Notice of Dispute filed during the life of the case? If more than one, report on the last 107.

8. Reason for dispute
   See comments on unlitigated case sample for explanation of hierarchy.

9. Mediation applied?
   Was a Compensation Consultant involved in attempting to resolve any disputes in the case?

11. Reason for hearing
    There will usually be an application for hearing so this item is designed to discover who filed first, the employee or the insurer.

12. Date of agreement to redeem
    Record the date of Form 18.

18. Was hearing held?
    Include redemption hearings as yes. If no hearing held indicate whether due to voluntary acceptance of claim, dismissal, or other reason.

19. Date of hearing
    As indicated on Form 200 or 113.

25. Outcome of hearing
    According to judge's order. Accepted voluntarily means hearing took place but no order was issued.

Page 4

26. Appealed?
    Was there a Form 19 filed with Appeals Board? If so by whom?

33. Date of appeal hearing
    As indicated on transcript.

39. Outcome of appeal
    According to who appealed.

40. Case referred for vocational rehabilitation?
    Is there a record of referral?

41. Vocational rehabilitation program instituted?
    What was result of referral?

42. Second Injury or Dust Disease Fund involved?
    Any record of involvement by either special fund?

Page 5

As used in unlitigated case sample. If weekly compensation benefits paid on this claim, record information here. Otherwise, skip to page 6. For reason payments stopped record the proximate reason: i.e., (1) employee did in fact return to work, or (2) dispute developed (insurer filed notice of dispute or petition for determination of rights or (3) Form 102 filed with MD statement of fitness, or (4) specific loss payments completed or (5) other.

Page 6

1. Reason for lump-sum
   If any lump-sum payment made to claimant other than for catch-up of weekly benefits, indicate reason.

2. Total amount
   Give total dollar amount of lump-sum payment as indicated on Form 200, 113 or 108.

8. Legal fees
   Record portion of total allocated to Attorney's fees.

13. Medical Expenses
    Record portion of total allocated to medical expenses.

18. Net to plaintiff
    Record amount claimant actually received, net of above expenses and free from reservation below.

24. Award for medical expenses
    Record here any amount of award specifically reserved or tagged for past, present or future medical expenses.

29. Is claimant retired?
    This will be difficult as there is no specific question on any form. Best source for this information will be judge's salmon sheet or medical report. Do not guess, if there is

not a reasonable certainty given case records, record unknown.

30. Has claimant returned to work?
    Also difficult. May be indicated on Form 102. Again check salmon sheet and medical reports for statements.

31. Date of final return to work
    Final return if known.

37. Date of final Form 102
    There should be a 102 for every case where compensation was paid. Record date on the form.

43. Encoder
    As in unlitigated case sample.

W. E. Upjohn Institute   <u>Litigated Cases</u>
for Employment Research

MICHIGAN CLOSED CASE SURVEY

1 [| | | | | |]   Case identification #

_____ Name of injured employee

8 [| |] - [|] - [| | |]   Social Security Number

17 [|]   County (see codebook)

_____ Employer

19 [| | | | | | | |]   Self insured number

27 [| |]   Insurance Company number
If multiple insurer liability:

_____ Employer #2

30 [| | | | | | | |]   Self insured number

38 [| |]   Insurance Company number

41 [ ]   Total number of employers involved

42 [|] - [|] - [|]   Date of AFH

48 [|] - [|] - [|]   Served and Set

54 [|] - [|] - [|]   Pre-Trial Conference Date

60 [|] - [|] - [|]   Claimant Birthdate (month-day-year)

66 [ ]   Sex   (1) Male
                 (2) Female

67 [ ]   Number of dependents

68 [| |]   Weekly earnings at time of disablement ($)

71 [|]   Daily wage at time of disablement ($)

218

Card 2

1 ☐☐ - ☐☐ - ☐☐ Last day worked

7 ☐☐ - ☐☐ - ☐☐ Date of injury or disablement

13 ☐ Type (1) Personal Injury (2) Occupational Disease

14 ☐☐☐ Nature of injury or illness (see codebook)

17 ☐☐☐ Part of body (see codebook)

20 ☐☐ - ☐☐ - ☐☐ Date of injury or disablement

26 ☐ Type (1) Personal Injury (2) Occupational Disease

27 ☐☐☐ Nature of injury or illness (see codebook)

30 ☐☐☐ Part of body (see codebook)

33 ☐☐ - ☐☐ - ☐☐ Date of injury or disablement

39 ☐ Type (1) Personal Injury (2) Occupational Disease

40 ☐☐☐ Nature of injury or illness (see codebook)

43 ☐☐☐ Part of body (see codebook)

46 ☐ Form 100 filed on any of these injuries?
(1) No
(2) Yes, first injury
(3) Yes, second injury
(4) Yes, third injury
(5) Yes, multiple
(6) Unknown

47 ☐☐ - ☐☐ - ☐☐ Date of Form 100 (earliest if multiple)

53 ☐ Fatality? (1) No
(2) Yes

54 ☐☐ - ☐☐ - ☐☐ Date of death

60 ☐ Hospitalization? (1) No
(2) Yes
(3) Unknown

Card 3

1 ☐ Form 107 filed? (1) No
(2) Yes

2 ☐☐-☐☐-☐☐ Date of 107

8 ☐ Reason for dispute
(1) Injury or disability denied
(2) Work relatedness of disability denied
(3) Liability of insurer denied
(4) Continued disability disputed
(5) Degree of impairment disputed
(6) Other, Specify _____

9 ☐ Mediation applied? (1) No
(2) Yes

10 ☐ Outcome of mediation
(1) Dispute resolved without hearing
(2) Dispute maintained
(3) Other, Specify _____

11 ☐ Reason for hearing
(1) Petition for hearing by employee (Form 104)
(2) Petition for hearing by insurer (Form 104)
(3) Agreement to redeem (Form 18)
(4) Application for advance (Form 108)
(5) Other, Specify _____

12 ☐☐-☐☐-☐☐ Date of Agreement to redeem

18 ☐ Was hearing held?
(1) Yes
(2) No, accepted voluntarily - petition withdrawn
(3) No, dismissed for lack of prosecution
(4) No, Other, Specify _____

19 ☐☐-☐☐-☐☐ Date of hearing

25 ☐ Outcome of hearing
(1) Redemption approved
(2) Redemption denied
(3) Benefits awarded
(4) Benefits denied
(5) Accepted voluntarily - petition withdrawn
(6) Stipulated
(7) Advance approved
(8) Advance denied
(9) Other, Specify _____

220

26 ☐ Appealed?
        (1) No
        (2) Yes, by employee (Plaintiff)
        (3) Yes, by insurer (Defendant)

27 ☐☐ - ☐☐ - ☐☐   Date of Form 19

33 ☐☐ - ☐☐ - ☐☐   Date of appeal hearing

39 ☐ Outcome of appeal
        (1) Plaintiff affirmed
        (2) Plaintiff reversed
        (3) Defendant affirmed
        (4) Defendant reversed
        (5) Dismissed
        (6) Other, Specify _____

40 ☐ Case referred for vocational rehabilitation?
        (1) No
        (2) Yes

41 ☐ Vocational rehabilitation program instituted?
        (1) No
        (2) Yes

42 ☐ Second Injury or Dust Disease Fund involved?
        (1) No
        (2) Yes

Card 4   - 5 -

If weekly compensation benefits paid:

1 ☐☐☐ Combined weekly earnings (from Form 101)

4 ☐☐ - ☐☐ - ☐☐ Date first payment made

10 ☐☐ - ☐☐ - ☐☐ Date of initial Form 101

16 ☐☐☐ Initial weekly compensation rate ($)

19 ☐☐ - ☐☐ - ☐☐ Beginning date for compensation

25 ☐☐ - ☐☐ - ☐☐ End date for compensation

31 ☐☐☐ - ☐ Compensation duration (weeks-days)

35 ☐ Kind of disability
    (1) Total
    (2) Partial
    (3) Specific loss
    (4) Death

If more than one compensation period:

36 ☐ Number of separate compensation periods

37 ☐☐☐ Final weekly compensation rate

40 ☐☐ - ☐☐ - ☐☐ Beginning date for compensation

46 ☐☐ - ☐☐ - ☐☐ End date for compensation

52 ☐☐☐ - ☐ Compensation duration (weeks-days)

56 ☐ Kind of disability
    (1) Total
    (2) Partial
    (3) Specific loss
    (4) Death

57 ☐☐☐ - ☐ Total compensation duration (all periods)

61 ☐☐☐☐☐☐ Total weekly compensation paid (all periods--$)

67 ☐ Reason payments stopped
    (1) Returned to work
    (2) Dispute
    (3) Physician's report
    (4) Benefits expired
    (5) Other, Specify _____

If lump-sum payment made:

1 ☐ Reason for lump-sum
    (1) Redemption (Form 113)
    (2) Decision (Form 200)
    (3) Advance (Form 108)
    (4) Other, Specify _____

2 ☐☐☐☐☐☐ Total amount ($)

  8 ☐☐☐☐☐ Legal fees ($)

 13 ☐☐☐☐☐ Medical expenses ($)

18 ☐☐☐☐☐☐ Net to plaintiff ($)

 24 ☐☐☐☐☐ Awarded for medical expenses ($)

29 ☐ Is claimant retired?
    (1) No
    (2) Yes
    (3) Unknown

30 ☐ Has claimant returned to work?
    (1) No
    (2) Yes
    (3) Unknown

 31 ☐☐ - ☐☐ - ☐☐ Date of final return to work

37 ☐☐ - ☐☐ - ☐☐ Date of final Form 102

43 ☐ Encoder

W. E. Upjohn Institute
for Employment Research

MICHIGAN CLOSED CASE SURVEY

1
☐☐☐☐☐☐☐ Case identification #

_____ Name of injured employee

9
☐☐☐ - ☐☐ - ☐☐☐☐ Social Security Number

18
☐☐ - ☐☐ - ☐☐☐ Birthdate (month-day-year)

24
☐ Sex   (1) Male
         (2) Female

25
☐☐ - ☐☐ - ☐☐ Date of injury

31
☐☐ - ☐☐ - ☐☐ Last day worked

37
☐ Fatality?   (1) No
               (2) Yes

38
☐☐ - ☐☐ - ☐☐ Date of death

44
☐☐ Place of injury (county--see codebook)

46
☐ Hospitalization?   (1) No
                      (2) Yes
                      (3) Unknown

47
☐☐ Nature of injury (see codebook)

50
☐☐ Part of body (see codebook)

53
☐☐ Hours regularly worked per week

55
☐☐ ☐☐ Straight time hourly wage rate ($)

59
☐☐☐ Combined average weekly earnings ($)

_____Employer

62
☐☐☐☐☐☐☐ Self insured number

70
☐☐☐ Insurance Company number

73
☐☐ - ☐☐ - ☐☐ Date of Form 100

224

Card 2

1
☐☐ - ☐☐ - ☐☐ Date disability commenced

7
☐☐☐ Combined weekly earnings (for compensation rate)

10
☐ Number of dependents

11
☐☐ - ☐☐ - ☐☐ Date first payment made

17
☐☐ - ☐☐ - ☐☐ Date of initial Form 101

23
☐☐☐ Initial weekly compensation rate ($)

26
☐☐ - ☐☐ - ☐☐ Beginning date for compensation

32
☐☐ - ☐☐ - ☐☐ End date for compensation

38
☐☐☐ - ☐ Compensation duration (weeks-days)

42
☐ Kind of disability
    (1) Total
    (2) Partial
    (3) Specific loss
    (4) Death

If more than one compensation period:

43
☐ Number of separate compensation periods

44
☐☐☐ Final weekly compensation rate

47
☐☐ - ☐☐ - ☐☐ Beginning date for compensation

53
☐☐ - ☐☐ - ☐☐ End date for compensation

59
☐☐☐ - ☐ Compensation duration (weeks-days)

63
☐ Kind of disability
    (1) Total
    (2) Partial
    (3) Specific loss
    (4) Death

64
☐☐☐ - ☐ Total compensation duration (all periods)

68
☐☐☐☐☐☐ Total weekly compensation paid (all periods--$)

-3-

Card 3

1 ☐ Reason payments stopped
    (1) Returned to work
    (2) Dispute (Form 107)
    (3) Physician's report
    (4) Benefits expired
    (5) Other, Specify_____

2 ☐☐ - ☐☐ - ☐☐ Date of final return to work

8 ☐☐ - ☐☐ - ☐☐ Date of final Form 102

14 ☐ Form 107 filed?   (1) No
                        (2) Yes

15 ☐☐ - ☐☐ - ☐☐ Date of 107

21 ☐ Reason for dispute
    (1) Injury or disability denied
    (2) Work relatedness of disability denied
    (3) Liability of insurer denied
    (4) Continued disability disputed
    (5) Degree of impairment disputed
    (6) Other, Specify_____

22 ☐ Mediation applied?   (1) No
                      (2) Yes

23 ☐ Outcome of mediation
    (1) Benefits continued or resumed
    (2) No further benefits paid

24 ☐ Case referred for vocational rehabilitation?
    (1) No
    (2) Yes

25 ☐ Vocational rehabilitation program instituted?
    (1) No
    (2) Yes

26 ☐ Encoder